THE ECHOES – LIFE & IMAGINATION : IMPRINTS OF THE OBLIVION

THE LITERATI

Made with ♥ on the Notion Press Platform
www.notionpress.com

To the seekers of stories,
The ones who dare to dream beyond the visible horizons,
This book is for you.

It is dedicated to the brilliant young minds
Whose pens have transformed thoughts into tales
And whose imaginations have built worlds beyond our own.

To the voices that whisper through these pages,
Your creativity is boundless, and your courage to share it is inspiring.
May your words soar, reaching readers far and wide,
Leaving imprints of wonder, curiosity, and reflection.

We extend our deepest gratitude to the mentors and guides
Who cultivated this creative spirit,
Who believed in every spark of potential,
And nurtured the stories into existence.

This anthology stands as a celebration of collective imagination,
Of young authors finding their voice,
And of a community that fosters growth and creativity
With unwavering dedication.

May these words ignite more dreams,
More stories,
And more inspiration for generations to come.

Contents

Contents

Foreword

The written word has always been a timeless bridge, connecting ideas, experiences, and emotions across ages and geographies. In "THE ECHOES- Life & Imagination: Imprints of the Oblivion", this anthology emerges as more than just a collection of stories; it is a vibrant testament to the creativity, passion, and expressive power of young minds. Each story, crafted by students, reflects a profound journey—an exploration of the boundaries between reality and imagination, past and present, fact and fiction.

In these pages, you will find narratives that capture the essence of life in its myriad forms: tales of triumph and resilience, quiet reflections on love and loss, adventures beyond the stars, and introspections on the self. What binds these varied stories together is not only the creative spirit of the authors but also the collaborative effort that birthed this anthology. It is the result of months of dedication, revisions, discussions, and, most importantly, the belief that stories have the power to move, inspire, and transform.

This anthology represents the heart of our community—the synergy between mentors and students, where every word written is a shared achievement. The pages before you are a reflection of young minds growing into their literary voices, unafraid to dive into complex emotions, to imagine boldly, and to express freely.

We hope that as you delve into this collection, you too will hear the echoes of life, the whispers of imagination, and the imprints left by each unique tale. It is with immense pride that we present this work, knowing that it holds within it the promise of more dreams yet to be penned and more stories yet to be told.

Preface

The inspiration behind The Echoes – Life & Imagination: Imprints of the Oblivion was born from a shared vision to create a student-driven initiative at SARO Corporation. The aim was to offer young minds a platform to express their creativity and foster the talents of aspiring authors. This book is a manifestation of our dedication to nurturing creativity and encouraging others to embark on their literary journeys.

Each story in this anthology was independently written by students from classes 10 to 12. The diversity of these narratives reflects the unique voices and imaginative spirits of its contributors. Through this book, we hope to inspire readers to be bold, to explore the world beyond their immediate surroundings, and to build their own paths with courage and perseverance.

Of course, this project did not come without its own set of hurdles. From finalizing the title, theme, and coverage to managing the authors and stories, every step demanded careful attention and collaboration. It required immense dedication, teamwork, and perseverance from everyone involved.

As you turn the pages of this anthology, we hope you find inspiration in the stories and feel empowered to chase your dreams with the same courage and determination.

Acknowledgements

Creating The Echoes – Life & Imagination: Imprints of the Oblivion has been a journey of passion, creativity, and learning, and it wouldn't have been possible without the unwavering support and dedication of many. This anthology is a true reflection of the talent and imagination of young minds, and we are deeply grateful for the opportunity to bring their stories to life.

We would like to express our heartfelt gratitude to everyone who supported this initiative. Their belief in nurturing creativity has given us the space to dream, explore, and create something meaningful. The valuable feedback and encouragement we received have been the foundation upon which this project was built.

We would also like to acknowledge the tireless efforts of the student Editorial Board, whose commitment to ensuring the quality of this anthology has been truly inspiring. Their careful rectification of each submission, while preserving the original essence of the stories, has made this collection a piece of work we are all proud of.

To all the student authors who contributed their stories to this anthology, thank you for sharing your imaginations and courage with us. Your work is a testament to the limitless creativity and potential that thrives within each of you. We hope that through this book, your stories will inspire many more to explore the art of storytelling.

Lastly, to the student volunteers who dedicated their time and energy to making this initiative a success, your hard work behind the scenes has not gone unnoticed. You have been the backbone of this project, and for that, we are truly grateful.

The Editorial Board

Dear Readers,

It has been an exhilarating journey to bring The Echoes – Life & Imagination: Imprints of the Oblivion to life. When we first envisioned this anthology, our goal was simple: to provide a platform where individuals could express their creativity and share their stories with the world. What we didn't anticipate was the immense depth, diversity, and brilliance that would emerge from the submissions. Every story has added its own unique flavor to the collection, and it's been our privilege to witness such exceptional talent.

As an Editorial Board, we have not only curated but also shaped the final collection, ensuring that every piece retains the essence of the author's voice while offering a polished, reader-friendly experience.

This anthology is a reflection of the creativity that thrives within young minds. It is also a testament to the collaborative spirit that made this project possible—authors, editors, and supporters all working together with a single purpose: to celebrate storytelling.

As we hand over this anthology to you, we hope you find as much joy in reading these stories as we did in crafting this collection. We invite you to get lost in the worlds created by our peers and perhaps even consider what stories you might one day share with the world.

With gratitude,
The Editorial Board

Aditi Priya | Anwesha Mishra | Avani Gujrati|
Ayush Kumar | Ayushman Malviya | Ishit Jaiswal |
Kumari Prachi | Saksham Kumar | Samriddhi Mishra |
Samriddhi Tanwani | Tanya Bairoliya | Vedika Mishra

Prologue

There are moments in life when the ordinary collides with the extraordinary, when fleeting thoughts give birth to vivid stories, and when silence gives way to voices too powerful to be ignored. It is in these moments that we find the genesis of art — and this book, The Echoes – Life & Imagination: Imprints of the Oblivion, is a reflection of those very moments. Within these pages lies the work of young dreamers who have taken their first steps toward the vast horizon of literature, each contributing a part of their soul to this collection.

This is not just a book. It is a meeting ground for countless emotions, an open stage for budding authors who dared to share the world as they see it, feel it, and dream it. Their stories are a testament to youthful curiosity, to the hunger for understanding, and to the magic that only words can conjure. These writers, in their formative years, have found the courage to unlock the doors to their imaginations, inviting you into realms where reality and fantasy entwine, where the known meets the unknown.

As you dive into these stories, you will sense the undeniable pulse of raw creativity. The themes are diverse, yet they are bound by a common thread — the pursuit of expression. Each narrative carries with it a voice that is unfiltered, honest, and uniquely its own. You will find tales that spark wonder, characters that leave their marks, and endings that linger in your thoughts long after the final page.

But perhaps the greatest gift this anthology offers is its reflection of youth itself — bold, restless, uncertain, and infinitely hopeful. It is a reminder that the most profound ideas often come from those who are still discovering their place in the world. Through the stories in this book, you will glimpse into the hearts and minds of a generation that is still shaping itself, yet has already begun to grasp the complexities of life and imagination.

This anthology is more than the sum of its parts. It is the spark of something greater, a collection of voices that will, in time, grow louder and clearer. What you hold in your hands is just the beginning. A beginning filled with promise, passion, and the unwavering belief that stories — like the people who tell them — can change the world.

Welcome to The Echoes. Let the journey begin.

Note

Fiction

As you turn the pages ahead, prepare to journey into the realms of imagination. These stories are born from the minds of budding authors, weaving tales that defy reality and venture into the fantastical, the mysterious, and the extraordinary. Each piece invites you to suspend disbelief, dive into the unknown, and embrace the magic of storytelling.

A gentle caution: The stories within these pages are purely works of fiction. Any names, places, or incidents mentioned are products of the authors' imagination. No actions depicted are to be recreated in classrooms,homes or elsewhere. These tales do not endorse or promote any form of crime, violence, or wrongdoing. Enjoy the creativity responsibly!

Shadows of Eastfield

About the Author: Aaditya Sharma
My name is Aaditya Sharma, and I hail from Haryana. I have a diverse range of interests, particularly in coding, which I'm currently learning, and in developing rocket models. My passion for biology enhances my understanding of the natural world. I thrive on hands-on projects that challenge me, and I am eager to explore my passions and make meaningful contributions as I embrace new experiences.

*****

On a warm summer morning, the sun casts a golden glow over the sleepy town. It was 10 a.m., and I sat in my usual spot—an old armchair by the bay window of my modest office. Sunlight filled the room as I immersed myself in The Alchemist, enjoying the peaceful silence only a small town like Eastfield could offer. I slipped by until my phone's soft chime broke the quiet. Detective Daniel. We had worked on countless cases together. He was one of the few I could trust, but his calls rarely meant good—usually a new case that would disrupt my peace. Before I continue, I'm Aiden, a private investigator in Eastfield. Locals call me "The Sleuth of Eastfield," a nickname I'm not fond of. In my line of work, fame is risky; the more people know your name, the harder it is to uncover hidden truths. Anonymity is far more valuable than recognition. When the phone rings with another case, it all feels the same. I had a feeling this call would lead to one of those days. Daniel's raspy voice carried urgency: Another murder! I grabbed my things and headed to the scene. The air smelled of blood. Daniel, standing among officers, greeted me with a smirk. "Let me guess—you were lost in The Alchemist when I called?" I chuckled. "You know me well." Despite my desire for peace, the pull of the chase always brought me back. "So, what's the situation?" I asked, feeling the familiar mix of curiosity and excitement. As much as I craved peace, the thrill of solving a case has always attracted me. Daniel's expression grew serious. "This one's different." The anticipation buzzed through me. Whatever was beyond that yellow tape, it would demand everything I had. Daniel led me through a dim alley, his voice steady. "Male, 37 years old. Found dead this morning around 9:25 a.m. Looks like he was heading somewhere, but never made it." "Name?" I asked. "Thomas Douglas." He signaled two officers to lift the sheets. Thomas lay there, pale, his face frozen in horror. This made my blood run cold. This was no ordinary case. It echoed one of my first—a killer who strangled victims with a satin garment. I caught him, but it was too late. I'll never forget the lifeless eyes of those I couldn't save. Daniel noticed the color drain from my face as the memories surfaced. "You okay?" Daniel asked, concerned. I forced a smile. "Yeah," though the words felt empty. As they presented new evidence, I felt unsettled. "We found this plant near the body," Daniel said, holding a bag with a plant. "It doesn't match local vegetation—some think it's a cactus." "A fishbone cactus," I muttered. The odds of it showing up here were too slim for coincidence. Daniel raised an eyebrow. "How do you know so much about cacti?" I chuckled. "Studied them for a college project...." He nodded. "You should talk to Vivian Douglas, the victim's wife. She might hire you." "I'll head there now," I said, though anxiety gnawed at me. This case would stir up more than just a killer—it would dig up stories from my past. I arrived at the residence, a gleaming building too grand for such grim circumstances. Inside the marble lobby, I showed my ID to the receptionist. She nodded and directed me to the elevator. The ride to the floor felt longer than it should have, the tension in my chest. I walked down the plush hallway to a wooden door. I hesitated briefly before ringing the bell. The door opened to reveal a woman in her early thirties, though grief had aged her. Her tired eyes and dark circles showed she hadn't slept. I explained why I was there. "You're the Sleuth of Eastfield, right?" she asked, her voice hoarse. I nodded. She stepped aside, letting me in. "I need you to find out who did this. Please." I could see she was holding on to the last bit of hope. I assured her, "I'll do everything I can." She nodded her trust—or maybe her last bit of strength—evident. She hired me on the spot. As I stepped outside the apartment, I felt this case would be more than just a professional challenge—it would test my resolve, skills, and sanity. After finalizing the fee with Mrs. Douglas, I headed home, burdened by heavy memories. I stopped at the police station to verify Mrs. Douglas's alibi. Detective Daniel agreed to look into it, though his curiosity was evident. Once home, exhaustion hit me. I took a shower, trying to ease the tension, but it did little to calm my mind. I went to bed hoping for a good night's sleep, but around 2 a.m., Detective Daniel's call shattered the silence. His grim voice delivered news:

there was another murder near the city center. I jumped out of bed, quickly dressing as I asked, "Same M.O.?" "Yes," Detective Daniel confirmed. "You need to get down here." "On my way," I said, shaking off sleep. I drove to the scene, the city's dark streets a blur. When I arrived, flashing lights illuminated the area with an eerie glow. Navigating through officers, I approached the taped-off scene. The method was disturbingly similar—a satin cloth and an M1 Garand left behind. The sight of the rifle triggered painful memories of my college days when a friend's argument led to him using an M1 Garand to shoot me. The scar on my stomach was a constant reminder. Daniel was present during the aftermath of my shooting years ago. The look on his face showed he too was haunted by that day. The new case's similarities—the satin cloth, the M1 Garand, and the violence—felt like an echo from my past, suggesting a killer who knew my history and was using it as an inspiration. The growing sense of dread was overwhelming. It felt like a personal attack. I had shared the details with Vivian, who was furious, but I was equally confused about how I got entangled in this nightmare. Each murder felt like a personal assault, and I was struggling. Daniel, recognizing the strain, invited me to 'The Ale Mary', our regular bar. It was a brief respite from the horror, offering a moment of normalcy. Despite the temporary peace, the killer was still out there. Daniel knew when I needed a break. The bar, our usual haunt where we'd forged our friendship over countless nights. For Daniel, this bar was more than just a retreat—it was a reset. He thought I needed a moment to clear my head before facing the chaos again.The bartender, familiar with our orders, approached with our usual drinks—an Everclear for Daniel and an Old Fashioned for me. As we settled in, the hours passed, softened by laughter and shared memories. Daniel's joke about an old, drunken rant and a breakup with Evelyn pulled me momentarily away from my troubles. His laughter and teasing brought a slight warmth. But then Daniel's phone rang. His face drained of color as he answered. When he hung up, the gravity of the call was palpable—another body. The city's tragedies seemed endless. I signaled for one last drink, only to find the cheerful young bartender replaced by an older, weary man. When I asked about the young bartender, the older man mentioned he'd left a few hours earlier due to family troubles. A sense of unease settled in me, but I pushed it aside. Heading toward Eastfield University, the air grew heavier, hinting at the darkness to come. The scene was grotesque: a young college student bound in satin with a ball of the same material stuffed in their mouth. The sight of a MacGregor golf club nearby sent a chill down my spine, and old, painful memories surged back. I staggered outside, vomiting uncontrollably, my body shaking. It took two exhausting days to confirm everyone's alibi, and we found nothing. Each person we questioned had airtight stories, placing them away from the crime. The only break came when the killer's last victim escaped by jumping from a window and providing a vague description. Daniel and I were left feeling defeated. He slumped in his chair, reflecting our frustration. "We've cleared all the alibis," he said. "It's like grabbing the ends of a broken rope." I leaned back, contemplating. "The killer knows my secrets, but I'm private. I only open up when I'm... My thoughts drifted. Daniel's humor broke my concentration. "To get you talking, I'd need a barrel of drinks." That's when it hit me: alcohol. I jumped up, grabbing Daniel's shoulders. "Alcohol is the key! I talk when I'm drunk." Daniel's confusion turned to understanding. "So, we're looking for someone who's been around when you drink?" "Yes!" I felt a surge of adrenaline. "I only drink at The Ale Mary. The killer must have learned about me there." Daniel's brow furrowed. "But usually, I'm with you when you drink. I've already been ruled out. I was with you during the second murder." The excitement waned as reality set in. "If it's not you, then who else? There must be someone who's been watching, blending in unnoticed," I said, pacing. Daniel leaned in, thinking. "Maybe it's someone who's been around but didn't stand out, like a regular at the bar who could slip in and out." We exchanged a look, realizing we had a lead. The Ale Mary was now the point of the investigation. "Let's go," Daniel said, grabbing his coat. The usual clamor welcomed us, and the bartender, always cheerful, began preparing our drinks. Watching the bartender work, I decided to engage him casually. "Heard you've been dealing with issues," I said. "Anything serious?" He smiled reassuringly. "Not too serious. My mother's been ill, and balancing her care with work has been tough, plus finances." I sensed something was off despite the bartender's seemingly genuine response about his ill mother. I patted his shoulder sympathetically, wished him well, and left a generous tip, though a nagging feeling remained. As we settled into The Ale Mary, the bartender, true to form, prepared our drinks. After hours of reviewing details on previous murders, we discovered a recurring name: Morrigan Contra. It was time to investigate her. The next day, I stood before an old, weathered apartment building and climbed the creaky staircase to her door. When I rang the bell, a young woman with wide eyes answered. "Oh my God! The Sleuth of Eastfield! Can I get a selfie?" she exclaimed before snapping a picture. I was taken aback. "Uh... can I talk?" I said. Her enthusiasm dimmed. "I know! It's about the recent murders. How can I help?" she asked eagerly. "Yes. For starters, what's your relation to the victims? You're a common contact," I inquired. She hesitated. "We were friends," she said quietly. "You don't seem particularly upset," I noted. "Well," she said, "we weren't close. We were in a club I led, where we discussed murders and cold cases. We all look up to you and want to be like you." A club of aspiring detectives? Why would a killer target them, and what connection did this have to me? I asked, "How many were there?""Five," she replied.Three were victims, leaving Morrigan and one more person. The last person, Linda Smith, lived two blocks away."We need to get to her house now. You're coming with me," I said urgently. As Morrigan locked her door, I called Daniel to update him.Arriving at Linda's building, I saw her door ajar and feared the worst. I told Morrigan to wait outside for the police and entered cautiously.The apartment was silent. Moving through the rooms, I reached the bedroom and saw the bartender strangling Linda with a satin cloth. I burst into the room, startling him, whose eyes met mine with a twisted grin. "You found me earlier than I expected," he said with a chilling calmness. "I know who you are, Jonathan," I replied, keeping my voice steady. "Let Linda go, and we can talk. No one else needs to get hurt." Jonathan's eyes gleamed with as he tightened a satin cloth around Linda's neck and yanked it up to the ceiling fan. "NO!" I shouted, lunging to free her. As I fought to loosen the cloth, Jonathan struggled to pull me off. The room was a frenzy of fear, and I felt time slipping away. Then, the sound of police sirens pierced the chaos, bringing a glimmer of hope. Jonathan paused, his grin widening. "I don't regret anything," he said. "I did it for you." He made no sense, but there was no time to process. The sirens grew louder, signaling Daniel's presence. "Morrigan!" I shouted. "Put your hands on your head and run towards the police now!" Though pale and confused, Morrigan complied, running with her hands raised. I saw her reach Daniel, who signaled the snipers. Daniel counted down—three, two, one—and a gunshot, followed by silence. I used the momentary distraction to free Linda, pulling her to the paramedics. She was alive. Jonathan lay on the floor, unconscious from a tranquilizer dart. The police had subdued him. His last words, "I did it all for you," haunted me, but Linda was the immediate priority. It has been two days since Jonathan was sentenced. The city was calm, but I still had unanswered questions about his motives. Driven by curiosity, I decided to visit jail. Jonathan sat across from me, his unsettling calm I'd seen before. I expected excuses or justifications, but what he revealed was shocking. "I did it all for you," he said softly, as if speaking to a friend. "Remember? Did you come to the bar sad and alone? You said your life was dull without excitement. The problem was the city, so I gave you a challenge." My stomach churned as he continued. "You were my only friend, and I wanted to make your life thrilling. The club members had to go—they were detectives, and I didn't want anyone to replace you." Jonathan had turned my boredom into a deadly game, believing it was an act of friendship. He was sentenced to death, but the weight of his actions left me more unsettled than ever. Just then, my phone buzzed. It was Detective Daniel. Another case.I sighed, knowing what it meant. Jonathan might soon face his final punishment, but the world was far from safe. Evil never truly disappears, and danger is never far away.

CHAPTER TWO

We Are In This Together

About the Author: Aayushmaan Malviya
In the divine streets of Varanasi, under a starry yet hazy night sky, a loud cry echoed through the hollow corridors of the local hospital. A child was born, destined for greatness with a vision and a sense of responsibility. Aayushmaan Malviya has been an avid reader ever since he first stepped through the doors of Sunbeam Bhagwanpur's Senior School. From an early age, he became a certified speller and orator, experiences that played a pivotal role in nurturing his passion for literature.

*****

In the midst of life's trials, it seems that God tests his best knights without a second thought, burdening them with challenges that feel insurmountable. Time plays a cruel trick, leaving one in a state of waiting, hollowed out by grief as tears have run dry. While brothers once engaged in a game of hide-and-seek, their true positions remain hidden, shrouded in deceit. Once inspired by a cheerful bird that sang daily, now reduced to a lifeless form, it lies in the grasp of predatory forces. As others strategize in their own games of chess, I find myself merely a participant, striving for approval while struggling to set up my own shelter amidst the chaos.

Just a calm and breezy commencement to the day, slipping down some warm coffee in the backyard, awaiting the newspaper, since surfing is better than scrolling. The doorbell rang, I rested my demitasse on the escritoire, and my socks gently tickled my feet as I went down the corridor. Opening the mailbox, it felt like the most refreshing essence trapped me and I leaned into it, willingly. There was a new attachment alongside the newspaper. A letter, directed to my address, was from my home, my ancestral house where I lived before moving out. Pure maple manuscript pages, I instantly got the hang of the writer. Only my mother can write a letter in the era of video conferences.

10th Street Avenue

Strait Park,

Wellingham Alley

March 2nd 2026

Dear son,

I've been longing for you for eternity, I hope you are fine and doing a terrific job at work. It is probably the last letter I am composing, I've been sick for the last few weeks, and I am under constant surveillance of medical support, but these medicines can only block the way for a few days, otherwise, your father is calling me. Before I walk the stairs I want to see my son once.

Hope you can take some time out from the urban wind.

With my warmest regards,

Your mother.

The pandemonium was febrile. My tears couldn't handle my distraught but they tried their very best. It was time for me to head back to my roots. I swept away the dust from my portmanteau, packed my life in it, and made a run for the bus.

The fresh air, the raw streets with hearts of gold. I, for a moment, forgot my purpose. All of my crumbled confidence and trepidation wafted up in the air. Even though it was a remote vicinity, the experience was incredible. While I was delved into my own nostalgia, a woman, with a creaky voice and a slightly bent back, but flawless hair patted my shoulders.

"I missed you so much. I am just hanging on a cliff with my hopes clinged on your arrival. I wanted to meet you once before I break ties from the earthly abstracts."

The room consisted of just the two of us, but the memories and versatile emotions left no corner vacant. I looked over my childhood draped over the wall. We spent the night with tranquillity, immersed in the past, I heard some bellows which reminded me of the wolves that used to protect us during the night, I comforted myself in the warmest blanket, but it felt like the urban wind had frozen my equipment. It seemed like the howls had no intention of hitting the skids, so I clustered some pebbles to ensure that they maintained a distance from our house. The cold breeze shuddered my spirit but something had to be done. The wooden doors of our house were opened to the startling visuals of a crew of men with the most expensive arms all locked and loaded. I rushed back to my house to ensure that my mother did not wake up. " Why are you trembling?" She said in a faint voice with her eyes closed, I didn't respond. The night darkened and finally a void was suspended in the air. The dawning sun endeavoured and carved out the greatest challenge. When the clock struck noon, a dozen or more men rusted the town hall, announcing that they had held the town hostage and acts of repulsion wouldn't reap fruitful outcomes. All of us were ransacked into an old library, with no food, no water whatsoever, just the one gallon of soda stationed near the gate. I was tensed about my mother's state, her health was slandering, and all this escalated her pulse above the hundred. I calmed her down but for how long? We were indefinitely trapped in this bunker of death with absolutely no inkling of the future.

The mendicants of Mercy,
Dragged into the null and void.
The bunker turned into the innocent's penitentiary,
People just scrolling it down on their Droid.

Five days went by, every second felt like an hour, and now the terrorists had to do what they did. They broke into the scene and shot one down in front of the gate as a message to the media and the government. The trepidation resonated with our souls. Our throats were slit, and the sounds of birds flapping away incarcerated our senses, every five to ten days, they came in, shot one, and went back. It felt like we were just toys to them. I tried to keep my mother calm but the only words she would say incessantly were "They are going to kill us." My heart was torn apart into fragments. A month passed, and her dilapidation crept up on my senses. We were sitting in the puddle of blood that once rushed into the nerves of our brothers. I was just feeding my mother her medicines with the help of the soda and keeping her distracted with the ostentatious abstracts when a couple of guys stormed in. The gates creaked open and the dark room was illuminated, I saw hope in that light as we were finally set free. My mother and I finally inhaled the air of freedom. A sense of tranquillity rushed past my soul as I tossed a look upon my mother to finally witness her smile, which I missed for a whole month, but her expression was contrary to my expectations, her eyes were shut, and the Sun rose.

After the cremation of her choice, I went back to my home. Which was just a piece of land now. When I looked at the past, it was dark. The cataclysmic events of the last month left a drastic impact and an everlasting scar. While I was sitting on the bed where she would tuck me to the blanket and sing me lullabies, I heard the knocking of the door, picking up the piece of cardboard that had my illustration with another woman, I mustered all my courage and opened the door. The neighbours were clustered on the street.

"We are in this together."

CHAPTER THREE

The Flames of Destiny

About the Author: Aditya Bhardwaj
I'm Aditya Bhardwaj, and my journey as a creator began with Harry Potter, which ignited my imagination and inspired me to write my own stories. Art has always been central to my identity, whether I'm composing music on my Casio or sketching. Each medium fuels my passion for storytelling, enabling me to explore worlds beyond reality. Currently, I'm crafting narratives that embody the magic I've always discovered in art, driven by a desire to create something meaningful.

*****

It began with the smallest of tremors. It felt as though the earth had drawn a breath and held it in. The traders and workers didn't bother, and apparently, they didn't sense it. Lucius did, of course, as it was his habit to inform everyone, "The earth never trembles without reason...". The tremors happened again today...

"Oh, come on, you are always focused on these trembles; give it a rest... God reminds us that a single seed does not yield a harvest, and the fleeting concerns do not birth greatness. Strive for what endures, and let the trivial fall away.' The people would say.

Lucius continued to work in the fields, still wondering what these signals from God meant. Was this his illusion, or was God showing his wrath? A question that had always eluded his understanding. "Anyways, the field is ploughed; I must go home at once. The sky is getting darker."

Working in Pompeii's fields was a mesmerizing experience, often described as "heaven on earth." Shepherds guided flocks, children played in meadows, and the golden sunlight bathed vineyards and olive groves. Hunters roamed fields encircled by volcanic mountains, with the Sarno and Silarus rivers winding through the breathtaking landscape.

As Lucius returns to his home, he encounters a familiar voice from behind. "Lucius!" it said, full of energy that broke through his thoughts.

Lucius looked up, and there she was, Livia, his sister. She carried a basket full of herbs and looked similar to Lucius except that while Lucius' brows were strong and straight, giving his face a grounded, reassuring quality, Livia's slender, arched eyebrows lent her an air of subtle expressiveness, as though her emotions were always just beneath the surface, ready to reveal themselves with a flicker of her gaze. "You're late. You were supposed to show up before sunset; I've been waiting!"

"The fields demand it. Anyway, why are you out here so late?"

"Nothing much had to get herbs from the fields. And the fields attract me just the same as they do to everyone."

"True. Anyways, did you notice the tremors today?"

" Tremors? No." She thought for a moment and then recalled excitedly. Lucius almost jumped. "But I did see smoke coming from Mount Vesuvius."

"Smoke? I knew something was wrong with these frequent tremors."

"Why are you worrying so much? It's just smoke, and it's not like smoke will engulf you," she said reassuringly. "Let's get back home; I've made tea for us."

"But... Okay."

As they walked in the narrow, winding streets of Pompeii, a figure arose from the shadows. He was dressed in priestly robes and looked as though he had seen horrors beyond comprehension. Mad with fear, he cried, "Lucius! Livia! Stop mortals, for I have something to tell you."

"Father Servius the mad priest, eh? Let's keep walking," said Livia, unbothered by Father Servius.

"No. I think it's something important; let's hear him out."

"Yes, yes, mortal, yes. Come here!" commanded the mad priest.

"What troubles you, Father?"

Suddenly, his eyes were covered in a fiery aura, as though it were on fire. He raised his arms in the air and started speaking uncontrollably...

"When the earth trembles and the sky darken. Fire and ash will consume the city of gold. Beware the lion's roar, for it will signal the end of Pompeii. Beware, for the god of fire has awakened from his sleep after 37 years... A boy shall be born on the 13th of February, and he shall be the Messiah of Pompeii." With this note, the mad priest stopped and dropped to the ground on his knee, uncontrollably panting heavily and gasping for air.

"Father Servius, are you alright?" said Lucius in utter horror.

"Let me get some water," said Livia, and she began to run.

"That won't be required," said Father Servius, and suddenly his fiery aura disappeared. "Why are you here, Lucius and Livia? Get on with your work! Off you both!"

"What?" the cousins replied, confused.

"Go!!" screamed the mad priest, and both of the cousins hurried off away from the street.

"What do you think all of that was about?" asked Livia once they got out of the street.

"I think it was some sort of prophecy... The fire god has awakened, and the lion roars—a boy born on 13ᵗʰ February. I think it's about the future of Pompeii; why do I think he meant destruction when he said so? Wait a minute. A boy was born on the 13ᵗʰ of February; that's exactly when I was born. He mentioned the boy's supposed to be the Messiah. It can't possibly be me, can it?"

"Calm down, Lucius; what makes you think you are the Messiah? And are you seriously going to believe what that mad priest says?"

"But his eyes... They were not his; I think he was possessed or something. It wasn't him who delivered that prophecy; it was someone else."

"Whatever, he may have used some of his old tricks to confuse us."

"The lion's roar..." Lucius murmured inquiringly at the words.

They reached their home, which was a big cluster of bricks and mud running everywhere. A small porch framed the entrance, where worn wooden chairs sat—often used for watching the sunset or sharing quiet conversations after long days in the fields. There was a hearth in the centre of the house, and above it hung a bundle of herbs giving a fresh scent of lavender, sage, and rosemary to the house. On a small table there was an oil lamp illuminating feeble rays of light and some small manuscripts, which Lucius liked to read after toiling hard in the fields. The kitchen was filled with the aroma of herbs and tea leaves, which Livia brought every week. The smell always attracted Lucius to his home; he used to crave those fresh loaves of bread along with some tea made from freshly plucked tea leaves after a long, tiring day. Directly opposite the hearth were two wooden bed frames, which provided enough comfort to sleep off a whole night.

"Did you notice the fiery aura in the priest's eyes?" asked Lucius, suddenly reminded of the incident.

"Drop it off, will you? Here, have your supper?" replied Livia frustrated as she handed over bread loaves, tea, and some olives to Lucius, who thought it best not to continue the topic considering Livia's anger at the moment.

After they ate their suppers, it was time to doze off. Before long, the weight of the work overtook Lucius and his thoughts faded into a quiet stillness.

Lucius was now standing in a deserted land, and ahead of him he could see Mount Vesuvius. He could see ashes and trickles of a fiery hot substance. He could see some people in the form of vapor running and disappearing into the air before Lucius could say something. He finally realized he was standing in his field, but it looked so different—as if all its life had been drained out of it. It looked pale and unhealthy. In the form of vapor, he saw a devilish figure arise out of Mount Vesuvius breathing fire everywhere, and finally Lucius heard it—the lion's roar, the voice of Mount Vesuvius. It was the most frightening experience in Lucius's life.

"Run for your lives, mortals!!" screamed the mad priest, and panic arose amongst everyone. But the fire was too quick; it engulfed half of Pompeii and was heading towards

Lucius, raging and hasting.

And suddenly, he woke back to life.

"Livia, Pompeii's going to burn soon! I saw it all in my dream!" said Lucius panic-stricken.

"Another dream? Said Livia, raising an eyebrow, and her lips curled into a half smile. "Again, about smoke and gods sending cryptic messages? You've had these before too; I don't think it's of any importance now."

"It was different this time. I saw Pompeii—our home—getting destroyed. I heard the lion's roar just like in the prophecy, and frequent small tremors were occurring just like I notice every day," said Lucius, dead serious, trying to prove that the prophecy is true to Livia.

"Well," said Livia, noticing the fear in her voice, and she stopped reassuring Lucius. This time, she said, "Do you think we should ask the mad priest about this?"

"We should".

"Then let's not waste any more time; I too felt tremors today."

They headed out of their house in search of Father Servius. The air was chill, but it wouldn't be for much longer. It was a common day for the merchants and farmers who were working tirelessly in their fields. One could yet again see children, this time trying to climb an oak tree. These little moments of happiness are what motivated Lucius to save the city, or at least its people.

At last, after walking for about half an hour, they were able to find Father Servius, sitting in an alley, apparently talking to himself, but one could never guess what he was up to.

"Hey, Father Servius! I've got something important to tell you," said Lucius yet again in a deadly serious tone.

" Important? What's so important in your life that you feel it's worthwhile to confide with me?" asked the mad priest and continued murmuring to himself.

"Yesterday, you might not be aware of it, but you revealed to us a prophecy. It was, undoubtedly, about the end of Pompeii. You mentioned that the lion's roar will signal the end of Pompeii, and a boy born on the 13th of February, who is probably me, shall be the saviour of Pompeii. What's more interesting is that I had a dream in which I heard the lion's roar and the voice of Mount Vesuvius, and I saw Pompeii—my home—getting demolished under the lava. What do you think of all this?" concluded Lucius.

" No! That means I was possessed... by the fire god. He burns everything he touches, even my mind! How was I not aware of it?" said the mad priest, irritated. "But anyways, a dream? The gods speak to you as well? Perhaps we share something in common. Perhaps they have chosen you as well for their madness, as they have cursed me. Or no. It may be a warning from the fire god. He does not lie; we are doomed, Lucius and Livia, doomed! "

"What do you mean? Can't we stop it?" asked Livia

The mad priest started laughing hysterically and almost immediately dropped his voice to a whisper before speaking again. "Stop it? Your mortal dare to think you can stop it? You can't stop what has already started. Pompeii will burn, and there's nothing we can do about it! Lucius, You and I... are but embers in his grand blaze. And in the end... we'll all burn."

As the mad priest concluded, there was a strong tremor in the earth, perhaps the strongest one they had encountered so far.

"Run mortals! It has already begun," said the mad priest, laughing madly.

"Lucius, what do we do?" asked Livia, now on the verge of tears.

"We... We have to get all the people together. I don't know for what, but I have a gut feeling we'll be able to do something together." said Lucius panic-stricken.

The whole ground was shaking hard; people were running around with their children. This was already not looking good.

"Hey you, HEY STOP! Get over here!" screamed Lucius, begging people to come together. But no one listened.

"I think we should ring the temple bells to attract them!" suggested Livia.

Lucius, without further ado, rushes through the crumbling streets and falling debris. His heart starts to race as he realizes the gravity of the situation. He reaches inside one of the temples in the countryside, the "heaven on earth," as he used to call it.

Quickly, he grabs the rope and pulls it with all his strength. The bell's sound cuts through the deafening chaos. The sound was otherworldly, sharp, and clear. "Gather in the temple; there's safety here!!" screamed Lucius at the top of his voice. This already started attracting many people, and they started to gather in the temple. In a moment or two, the temple was full of people.

"You fool! Do you know the wrath of the fire god?! Do you think some stupid temple bells will save you?" intervened the mad priest. "We can probably --" but Lucius was never able to finish the sentence because he heard a huge crack in Earth as if it split open. The sky had started to turn red, the same red he saw in the mad priest's eyes. There were puffs of smoke arising here and there. The people had started getting out of the temple to check the situation; Lucius followed them, and what he saw was unimaginable. The fire god Kaldor had arisen out of Mount Vesuvius looking pleased because of something. His sheer presence made goosebumps arise in Lucius's whole body, and when The God spoke, it was as if he felt himself speaking.

"Well done, Lucius, mortal!" Spoke Kaldor in an ironically cold voice. "For you have done exactly as I intended you to do. You brought all of your people to their doom."

Panic arose at the sound of these words, and all of them started criticizing Lucius for gathering them. Lucius, however, tried to remain calm and replied, "That was a part of your plan? What less to expect from a god like you? A manipulator, a cheater, you don't represent the word divine!"

"You dare speak to me like that mortal? It was the deeds of you and your people that resulted in a punishment like this! You might not have noticed it, Lucius, but I did... I saw the greediness, selfishness, and sinister nature in every one of these people. I was watching patiently, waiting; perhaps they will change... perhaps they will cure the contagious disease of selfishness, but not anymore. You, Lucius, have only seen the good in people, seen this countryside as heaven on Earth. That's why you have no play in this, and I propose an offer to you: I intend to save you and your family, but Pompeii will turn to dust."

"Well, then the whole of Pompeii's my family. Will you save us all?"

"I won't at all!" replied Kaldor, irritated.

"Sire, there is no need for you to listen to this naive mortal! I think it is best for you to continue your plan and demolish Pompeii once and for all," intervened the mad priest again.

"I agree," replied Kaldor coldly. He started to form a fireball in his hand and was ready to demolish the whole of Pompeii with a mere fireball.

"STOP!" said Lucius boldly. He dropped a manuscript on the ground. Livia picked up the manuscript, and on the manuscript were scribbled the words.

"Run as far as you can from this place when I say 3. Don't look back after you start running."

"What is it mortal?" asked Kaldor.

"3!" screamed Lucius.

All of the people started running away as quickly as possible. There was chaos everywhere, and people were pushing each other, craving to escape. The mad priest also found it suitable to run away. Lucius remained where he was, but he took out a small relic out of his pockets.

"STOP MORTALS, WHERE DO YOU THINK YOU'RE GOING TO?" said Kaldor, enraged. He threw the fireball he had formed in his hand at the people; it travelled almost at lightning speed until eventually it was blocked by something.

On the ground stood Lucius, the sacred relic of Jupiter in his hands. Jupiter, the god who often protected the world in times of chaos. It was apparent now that hope had never died away.

"STOP IT, LUCIUS! HOW DID YOU GET THE POWER OF JUPITER?" Kaldor exclaimed.

"I stole that from your puppet mad priest. Every power you wield leaves a shadow, Kaldor. The very destruction you've unleashed will turn against you!" said Lucius.

The sky was filled with a royal blue colour, and a big figure of Jupiter stood beside Lucius. With the collective power, Lucius was able to stop Kaldor and the people from running away from the upcoming ordeal.

"I dedicated myself to Pompeii and its people. I hope that one day Pompeii will be recreated and it will flourish even better than it did today. This is the beauty of the "heaven on Earth.". I hope someday you'll realize, Kaldor, that you made a mistake destroying such a beautiful land. Until then, goodbye Pompeii and goodbye Livia. And with these words, Lucius was engulfed in the fire as the power of the sacred Jupiter relic ran out. With a bittersweet smile, Lucius left the world to reside in a better place.

Somewhere, much time later, Closing the manuscript titled "Here stood Lucius, the Messiah of Pompeii.". A historian sighs, looking out at the distant horizon, where the remnants of Pompeii lie, now silent and still. He murmurs to himself, "In the end, it was not the fire god's wrath that endured—it was Lucius' courage."

CHAPTER FOUR

The Shattered Bond

About the Author: Amritansh Rai

My name is Amritansh Rai, and I was born on December 6, 2007, in Ballia District. I completed my studies up to class 8 at Sunbeam School in Ballia, and I continued my education by enrolling in Sunbeam English School Bhagwanpur for class 9. I have a passion for traveling and exploring new experiences, and I aspire to pursue a career in MBA.

****

There are certain people in life you believe will never leave. You never entertain the thought because they're too deeply intertwined with who you are. For me, that person was Steve, my best friend. No, he wasn't just a best friend. He was my partner in crime, my anchor, the person who knew me better than I knew myself. We were inseparable, or at least that's what I thought. The moment we met, something clicked. We shared the same sense of humour, the same love for adventure, and an unspoken understanding of each other's thoughts and feelings. I could be completely vulnerable with him, and I thought he felt the same. We didn't have to explain ourselves; we just knew. He used to tease me a lot, to such an extent that I used to get mad at him, and then he used to apologize. He took care of me like a small baby and scolded me when I was wrong. But as they say, good things don't last long. Or at least that's what I believe. Somewhere along the way, things began to change. Or maybe it was me. I started depending on him more than I realized. His presence became my emotional compass, his approval, my anchor. When Steve was around, I was at peace. But when he wasn't... the silence became unbearable. I didn't even notice how much my world had started to revolve around him until it was too late. I had gotten attached. It happened suddenly. One day, I sent him a message like I always did. Nothing deep, just a casual "What's up, dude?" But his reply wasn't what I expected. It wasn't the usual banter, no funny quip. Instead, I got this: "I can't do this anymore. Don't contact me again. Leave me alone. I wish you all the happiness in your life." I stared at my phone, waiting for the punchline, but none came. I read it over and over, the words like knives sinking deeper each time. It didn't make sense. There was no fight, no warning, nothing. Just those cold, empty words. My fingers trembled as I called him. Straight to voicemail. I sent more messages, asking why and pleading for an explanation, but the silence was louder than anything I'd ever known. He was gone. Just like that. My best friend, my partner in crime, had walked away without giving me a reason. Days passed, then weeks. I tried to go through the motions of life, but everything felt wrong. My mind was in a constant loop of overthinking, replaying every moment we'd shared, every conversation, every joke. Had I done something wrong? Said something? I recalled each of our memories, searching for a clue, a hint as to what went wrong, but I found nothing. I focused on possibilities, hurting myself by what I did wrong. I took the blame on me. The silence was unbearable. I wanted to scream, to cry, to let out the hurricane of emotions tearing me apart from the inside, but no tears came. Nothing. Just a numbness that I couldn't shake. It was as if Steve had taken that part of me with him when he left. I used to believe in things like friendship, loyalty, and trust. I thought the bond we had was unbreakable. But now I wasn't sure if I believed in any of these things again at all. How could I, when the person I trusted most cut me off his life without even telling me why? I told him what hurt me the most, and he did the same; he also left me alone and broke my trust. I'd always be the kind of person who valued deep connections. I didn't have many friends, but the ones I had meant everything to me. And Steve? He was the closest thing I had in my life after my parents. I used to think we'd be friends forever. That's how it always felt—until it didn't. At first, I told myself that he'd come back. Maybe he just needed some space. Maybe I was too clingy; that was too much. Maybe that was it. So, I waited. I kept the hope intact. Days turned into weeks, and I kept hoping, checking my phone, waiting for him to reach out and say it was all a mistake. But he never did. And the hope broke. The more time passed, the more I realized that he was gone. Not physically, of course. He was still out there, living his life, laughing, existing—but without me. I was nothing to him now. And that realization tore me apart more than I ever put into words. People around me started to notice the change. They asked if I was okay, and I lied. I told her that I was fine because, how could I explain the truth? How could I tell them that the person I had trusted most, the one who knew me better than anyone else, had just disappeared without warning? I felt humiliated. Abandoned. Like, I was not worth an explanation. And the worst part? I couldn't even be angry. I wanted to be. I wanted to scream his name, curse him, and hate him for what he'd done. But I couldn't; how could I hate that person who meant the world to me at one point and maybe still did? How do you ever come to accept the fact that your best friend is no longer your friend? Even if he hurt me, I still can't. All I could do was sit with the weight of the emptiness he left behind, overthinking every moment and every word. I started avoiding people. I withdrew into myself, convinced that if he could leave so easily, so could anyone else. I stopped trusting. Stopped believing in the idea of friendship. After all, how could I believe in something so fragile? Something that could be ripped away in an instant, without any warning, without any closure? Nights were the hardest. I could lie on the bed, staring at the ceiling, my thoughts spiralling out of control. I replayed every conversation we ever had, searching for answers that didn't exist. My mind was twisting itself into knots, trying to understand why someone who promised to always be there could just vanish like that. I stopped crying. The pain went too deep for tears. Instead, it settled into a dull, constant ache that never really went away. It was like a part of me had been cut off, but the wound never healed. And every time I thought about him, it was like ripping it open again. People told me that attachments hurt a lot, but I didn't listen that time, and now I'm here, shattered and broken as hell. The world kept moving around me, but I was stuck. People would talk about their friends, their laughter, their stories, and I'd sit there, numb, wondering if I'd ever be able to trust anyone like that again. I couldn't even bring myself to say his name anymore. It hurt too much. The memories of him felt like they belonged to someone else, to a version of me that no longer existed. Because I wasn't the same anymore. I wasn't me anymore. Steve had taken that part of me with him, and I didn't know how to get it back. That day I didn't just lose my friendship, but more than that, I lost my old self. That jolly go-to sunshine boy who turned into a quiet, serious human to exist.

CHAPTER FIVE

The Lost Soul

About the Author: Ananya Ojha
My name is Ananya Ojha, and I am an 11th-grade student at Sunbeam English School Bhagwanpur. I have a passion for creative writing and storytelling. This is my first work, and I am excited to share my imagination with readers.

*****

Naksh was a sixteen-year-old boy, cherishing a simple, joyful life with his parents and beloved grandmother. His grandmother was the center of his world, and he, hers. She adored him deeply, and Naksh couldn't imagine a single day without her. Their bond was the kind that wrapped hearts in warmth, and their laughter often filled the house with life. But time was unkind—his grandmother had grown frail with age.

One fateful day, her health suddenly worsened. That day, the house was unusually quiet, with no one home except Naksh. Oblivious to her struggles, Naksh had his headphones on, immersed in his favorite music. Meanwhile, his grandmother was calling out his name, her voice trembling with urgency. Minutes passed before Naksh removed his headphones, hungry and headed to her room to ask about lunch. What greeted him instead was a horrifying sight—his grandmother lay pale and weak, struggling for breath.

Panic surged through him as he fumbled to call the doctor. But fate was cruel. By the time the doctor arrived, she had already left this world. When the doctor somberly remarked that calling him earlier might have saved her, Naksh felt his heart shatter into a million pieces. Tears streamed down his face as he collapsed to his knees, blaming himself for her untimely death.

His parents tried their best to console him, assuring him that her time had come and that he was not at fault. But Naksh couldn't let go of the guilt. His mind echoed with relentless thoughts: If only I had been there. If only I had listened. She would still be with me today. Her absence carved an unfillable void in his life, and he spent his days lost in her memories—her warm smile, her gentle hands feeding him, and the way she always made him feel special.

A month passed, yet Naksh refused to return to school. His parents eventually forced him to resume his routine, hoping it might bring him some solace. One day, while returning home from school, he ran into Rajiv, their friendly neighbor. Rajiv, a college student studying paranormal science, had always been someone Naksh admired. Rajiv sensed the boy's sorrow and invited him over that evening to share something intriguing.

When Naksh visited, Rajiv spoke of Phowa, an ancient Buddhist practice that allowed the soul to leave the body and transcend time. Naksh's curiosity was piqued. "Is there a way to reverse time?" he asked with a flicker of hope in his tear-streaked eyes. Rajiv handed him a book detailing the Phowa ritual but warned him sternly not to try it alone. Yet, desperate to see his grandmother again, Naksh ignored the warning.

The book described the ritual as most effective on Purnima—the night of the full moon. On that night, driven by his yearning, Naksh performed the ritual alone in his room. The next morning, his mother found him unresponsive. Despite all efforts, he wouldn't wake up. The doctor confirmed that Naksh had slipped into a mysterious coma, though all his test reports were normal. Days turned into weeks, and his parents were losing hope.

One day, while cleaning Naksh's room, his mother stumbled upon the strange book. Alarmed, she showed it to Rajiv, who immediately understood the situation. He rushed to his professor, Dr. Vinayak, an expert in paranormal studies. After examining Naksh, Dr. Vinayak revealed that Naksh's soul had ventured too far from his body and was now trapped. Worse still, a malevolent spirit sought to occupy Naksh's body, potentially wreaking havoc in the world.

Dr. Vinayak explained that to save Naksh, someone had to perform the Phowa ritual to retrieve his soul. Naman, Naksh's father, volunteered, despite the grave dangers involved. The professor warned that the spirit might attack him and that he had only two hours to succeed.

On the night of the next Purnima, the ritual began. As Naman's soul entered the otherworldly realm, he was engulfed by chilling darkness and the haunting echoes of cries and screams. Moving cautiously, he eventually found Naksh's soul shackled and lifeless. Freeing his son, Naman guided him back toward his body. But just as they neared it, Naksh's soul grinned wickedly and pushed Naman aside. Horror dawned—it wasn't Naksh's soul but the insatiable spirit.

Time was slipping away. Naman, now imprisoned by the spirit, felt despair creep in. Just as hope seemed lost, a radiant white light illuminated the darkness. When Naman opened his eyes, he found himself back in his body—and Naksh was awake too. Relief flooded the room, but confusion lingered. How had they both returned?

Later that night, Naksh stayed awake, still shaken by the experience. Suddenly, the same white light reappeared. Out of it stepped his grandmother, her presence ethereal yet familiar. With tears in her eyes, she embraced Naksh. "My dear child," she said, "you are not to blame for my passing. I have always been with you and always will be." She explained that she had guided Naksh's soul back and saved Naman from the evil spirit. With one last loving hug, she whispered, "I love you, my child. Be happy," and disappeared into the light.

Naksh felt a peace he hadn't known in weeks. Though his grandmother was gone, her love remained—a light to guide him through even the darkest times.

CHAPTER SIX

The Infinite Echoes of Stardust

About the Author: Astha

Astha is a 15-year-old space enthusiast with a passion for reading books on astrophysics and cosmology, which heavily influence her daily conversations. In her leisure time, she enjoys listening to music—especially Taylor Swift—stargazing, reading, and watching sitcoms like The Big Bang Theory and K-dramas. A true foodie at heart, she can't resist drooling over Chinese cuisine.lects this same spirit of innovation. She isn't just a human; she is an ironic conspiracy in herself.

*****

PART 1: The Flames of Infinity

"To burn is not to refute!" These were the anguished final cries of a lesser-known man engulfed by merciless flames—a martyr of science, a revolutionary thinker, and the eternal dreamer, Giordano Bruno.

It was in the brisk February of 1548, under the starry skies of Naples, Italy, that a boy was born into a world teeming with mysteries. His wide, curious eyes seemed to capture the glistening heavens above, and from a young age, an insatiable yearning to understand the universe pulsed through his veins. He was destined to question, to seek, and ultimately, to challenge the very foundations of the world he inhabited.

Raised amidst the devout teachings of the Catholic Church, young Bruno's early life revolved around faith and theology. His family, devout believers, ensured that their son embraced the doctrines of the time. At the tender age of 17, Bruno took his first significant step into the world of spiritual and intellectual exploration by joining the Dominican Order. Upon his initiation, he adopted the name Giordano, marking the beginning of his journey as a friar.

The monastery became his sanctuary of knowledge, offering access to the profound works of Aristotle, the revered thinker whose philosophies had shaped centuries of thought. Yet, as Bruno delved into Aristotle's teachings, a storm of questions began brewing in his young mind. The rigid geocentric model, which placed Earth immovably at the center of the universe, struck him as deeply limited. This worldview, endorsed by both Aristotle and the Church, failed to align with the expanding scope of Bruno's imagination.

During this time, the revolutionary ideas of Nicolas Copernicus began to reach Bruno's ears. Copernicus proposed a heliocentric model, placing the Sun at the center of the universe and depicting Earth as one of many planets orbiting it. While this perspective was radical, it still confined the cosmos within a finite framework. Bruno, however, found himself troubled by a deeper question: Could Earth truly be the only cradle of life? Could the Sun alone shine amidst a sea of eternal darkness?

On a gusty, restless night, Bruno felt an irresistible pull toward forbidden knowledge. He ventured into the shadows, where the secrets of the cosmos lay hidden. His trembling hands brushed away a thick layer of dust from an ancient, forbidden tome. Its title, barely visible under the dim light, read: *De Rerum Natura* by Lucretius (*On the Nature of Things*).

The brittle pages revealed an audacious vision of the universe. Lucretius, a Roman philosopher and poet, dared to imagine an infinite cosmos, boundless and eternal. He asked his readers to envision an arrow released into space, traveling ever onward. What if it struck a wall? Could another arrow be shot beyond it, challenging the idea of any boundary? Through this elegant metaphor, Lucretius argued for an infinite universe governed by material forces and natural laws. He urged humanity to embrace chance, Fortuna, and to reject fear of gods or death.

Bruno's heart raced as he absorbed these radical ideas. Each word seemed to illuminate a new facet of the cosmos, as though unveiling secrets hidden in the fabric of existence. The thought of a boundless, infinite universe exhilarated him. It was a revelation that resonated deeply with his own musings, affirming the belief that reality extended far beyond the confines of human perception.

But his reverie was abruptly shattered. A loud, menacing thud broke the silence, and Bruno looked up to find the stern faces of Church officials looming over him.

"Quick! Take that filthy book from him!" bellowed the head priest, his voice seething with rage. The sacred halls of the monastery, once Bruno's refuge, now echoed with condemnation.

"Young man," the priest continued, his tone dripping with disdain, "you are banished from the sacred grounds of our church for committing such a grievous sin! To question the truth we hold sacred is to align yourself with heresy!"

Bruno, clutching the book tightly, was cast out into the cold night. The gates of the monastery slammed shut behind him, severing his ties to the life he had known. Stripped of his vocation, his home, and his purpose, he wandered the streets of Naples.

The townspeople, once warm and familiar, now turned their faces away in disgust. Some whispered, others spat. To them, Bruno was no longer the bright young friar with a future; he was a heretic, a man who dared to defy the Church's authority. Yet, within Bruno's heart, a fire burned brighter than ever—a fire fueled by the boundless vision of the universe he had glimpsed.

That night, Bruno sought solace in the quiet embrace of a forest, longing for warmth. Dead, brown leaves blanketed the ground like nature's somber offering, while the faint trilling of cicadas provided an almost hypnotic lullaby. It was as if the forest itself conspired to ease him into a restful slumber, triggering his melatonin and lulling him into unconsciousness. One might assume that losing his home, reverence, and livelihood would devastate his spirit, but Bruno remained unfailingly optimistic. The revelations he had gleaned from forbidden books filled him with an exhilarating sense of purpose.

Gazing up at the vast expanse of stars, he marveled at what he believed to be both the creation of God and the masterpiece of nature. As he slipped into sleep, his dreams transported him to a world of infinite wonder.

In his dream, Bruno floated effortlessly away from Earth and into the infinite void. He saw our solar system laid bare before him, the planets revolving with cosmic grace around the Sun. But as he ventured further, it became clear that the solar system's edge was merely a horizon. Beyond it, countless other suns accompanied by their own Earth-like planets stretched into eternity.

There was no center, no end, only boundless infinity. Bruno beheld this grand cosmic tapestry with awe, as if he had touched the divine. It was a moment of unparalleled revelation—a purpose ignited within him. He thought, *Am I more fascinated by the universe above us or the one within us?*

As dawn broke, rays of sunlight pierced through the trees and illuminated Bruno's face. The warmth stirred him awake, filling him with renewed hope—a hope that he believed could transform humanity's understanding of existence.

Eager to share his vision, Bruno attended a lecture at Oxford, where he addressed an audience of scholars:

"Greetings, gentlemen. Today, I, Giordano Bruno, stand before you to share a vision—a revelation bestowed by the Almighty. In my dream, I floated through the vast darkness of space, where up and down ceased to exist, and the center was a mere illusion. I saw our Sun as just another star, and the stars were other suns, each accompanied by Earths like our own. This boundless universe is a testament to the infinite creativity of God. To witness this immensity was like falling in love."

His impassioned words, however, were met with murmurs of dissent. The room erupted in jeers and mocking exclamations.

"What a fool!" someone scoffed.

"Everyone knows there is only one Earth," declared another man, his tone dripping with arrogance.

"What everyone knows is wrong!" Bruno retorted, his voice ringing with conviction. "Our infinite God created a boundless universe filled with countless Earths!"

The audience's derision intensified. Bruno was pelted with tomatoes and slippers, his ideas dismissed as heretical ramblings. He was banned from speaking at future gatherings of the learned elite.

His defiance did not go unnoticed. Soon, Bruno found himself ostracized by the Catholic Church, expelled from Switzerland, and barred from public discourse. Stripped of his platform, he wandered the streets, his faith in humanity eroding. Yet, even in the face of rejection and exile, Bruno never doubted the truth of his beliefs.

Eventually, the Church's wrath caught up with him, and he was imprisoned. For seven long years, he languished in a cell, gazing at the stars through a tiny hole in the wall. The celestial lights, unchanging and eternal, became his only solace. They reminded him of the vast canvas upon which all of humanity existed—trees painted upon an infinite masterpiece.

On February 17, 1600, Bruno was led to Campo de' Fiori, where he was burned alive by the Roman Inquisition. His final cries echoed through the square: *"To burn is not to refute!"* The flames consumed his body, but they could not extinguish his ideas. His sacrifice became a symbol of resistance against ignorance and oppression.

Bruno's legacy might have been buried with his ashes, but the universe had other plans. A decade later, Galileo Galilei peered through a telescope and discovered a planetary system orbiting the Sun, affirming the heliocentric model Bruno had so fiercely defended.

Today, Giordano Bruno is remembered not just as a martyr of science but as a visionary who defied the constraints of his time. He dared to challenge orthodoxy, to question the boundaries of knowledge, and to dream of a cosmos unbounded. This humble tale is a tribute to one of history's most courageous thinkers—a man who gazed into infinity and refused to look away.

PART 2: The Cosmic Graveyard

The night at the English coast was a canvas of shimmering water, softly lapping at the shore. William Herschel and his ten-year-old son strolled along the cool, damp sand. The rhythmic murmur of the waves composed a tranquil lullaby, blending harmoniously with the vast, starlit sky above. The boy's curious gaze lingered on the glimmering stars reflected in the dark water. Above them, the moon reigned supreme, its silvery light overpowering the faint twinkle of countless stars scattered across the heavens.

A gentle zephyr whispered through their clothes as William interrupted the quiet, pointing toward the eastern sky. "Look there, son," he said. "That's Sirius, the brightest star in the night sky."

The boy followed his father's gesture, tilting his head to gaze at the shining orb. Its brilliance seemed almost alive against the inky blackness.

Breaking the silence, the boy asked hesitantly, "Father, do you believe in ghosts?"

William paused, then replied with a slight smile, "Why yes, son, I do!"

The boy's eyes widened with astonishment. "Y-you do?"

"Well, not the human kind of ghosts—no, not at all. But look up at the sky, at the stars."

"The stars, Father? I don't understand."

William crouched to his son's level, his voice soft yet brimming with wonder. "Every single star you see out there is as big as our Sun, or even bigger. Now, close your eyes for a moment and imagine how far you'd need to go to make our Sun look as tiny as those stars. You see, the light from the stars travels faster than anything else, but it isn't infinite—it takes time. For the nearest stars, it takes years for their light to reach us. For others, centuries. And for some, millions of years.

"By the time their light reaches us, those stars may already be gone. What we see now are not the stars themselves but their ghosts—the echoes of their past, traveling across the vastness of space and time."

The boy's eyes sparkled with wonder as he stared into the infinite night. For a moment, the world seemed to hold its breath.

"John," William continued gently, "do you know who you were named after?"

"No," the boy said, his voice barely above a whisper.

"You, my dear son, are named after John Michell—an old and dear friend of mine. He was the first to propose the idea of 'dark stars.'"

"Dark stars?"

"Yes," William said, standing and gazing upward once more. "They may seem far away, but the answers you seek are always within reach—if you look closely enough."

The scene shifted to a crisp evening in the quiet village of Thornhill, Yorkshire. The air was alive with the faint chirping of crickets as John Michell, a revered clergyman, sat within the warm glow of his study. Though known as a man of God, Michell's thoughts often strayed to the cosmos and its infinite mysteries. His modest wooden house was filled with books and papers on Newtonian mechanics, astronomy, and geology. Ideas buzzed within these walls, worlds away from the tranquil English countryside beyond the creaking door.

A steaming cup of tea sat on the nightstand, its warmth fogging the nearby glass window. This simple ritual signaled a long evening of research and contemplation ahead. Michell's mind, however, was anything but simple. It roamed the universe, grappling with the fundamental truths of existence.

It was in this very study, surrounded by the whispers of the stars, that Michell pondered a revolutionary idea: the possibility of dark stars—celestial objects so dense that even light could not escape their grasp. Though centuries would pass before such objects would be confirmed as black holes, Michell's vision laid the foundation for future generations of stargazers and dreamers.

Back at the coast, the boy named John stood beside his father, absorbing the vastness of the sky. He couldn't have known it then, but the wonder sparked within him would ripple through time, connecting him to the legacy of Michell and others like him. Together, they carried the torch of curiosity, illuminating the boundless mysteries of the universe.

And so, under the shimmering tapestry of the stars, the story of discovery unfolded—a reminder that every question, no matter how vast, begins with a single spark of curiosity.

Michell sat quietly in his worn wooden chair, the faint creak of its legs echoing through the still room. He reached for his steaming cup of tea, letting the warmth seep through his hands as he took a thoughtful sip. His mind was deep in contemplation, grappling with Newton's laws of motion and his groundbreaking works on gravity. The forces that governed the heavens, binding celestial bodies in an intricate dance, seemed to him both majestic and mysterious.

Michell's thoughts wandered to the nature of light itself. He knew that light had a finite speed and was composed of corpuscles—infinitesimally small particles with no mass and negligible size. He took another sip, his brow furrowing. If gravity could alter the trajectory of physical objects, why not the path of light as well? It was a radical notion, one that sent a chill down his spine despite the tea's comforting warmth.

The pieces of the puzzle began falling into place, each thought cascading into the next with increasing clarity. Michell leaned back in his chair, his eyes drifting upward to the twilight sky. The faint stars overhead seemed to beckon, urging him to delve deeper into this uncharted realm of ideas. He whispered to himself, "What if there is a star so massive that even its own light cannot escape its gravitational clutch?"

The concept of escape velocity— the minimum speed required for an object to break free from a celestial body's gravitational pull—came to mind. Michell imagined a star of unimaginable mass, so dense and powerful that the required escape velocity exceeded the speed of light. Such a star would exist, but its light would be trapped, rendering it invisible to the human eye.

His heart raced at the thought. A star that could not be seen but exerted its influence nonetheless—a ghost among the heavens. Without hesitation, Michell grabbed a piece of parchment and began scribbling furiously.

"The speed of light is finite, and if the escape velocity of a star is greater than that speed..." he wrote, his thoughts pouring onto the page like a torrent.

The realization struck him like a thunderclap. Such a star would be what he called a "dark star," a celestial entity so massive and dense that its immense gravitational pull rendered it incapable of emitting visible light. It would exist as a phantom in the cosmos, detectable only through its gravitational effects.

The room seemed to hum with energy as Michell worked late into the night, performing intricate calculations to determine the mass and density such a star would require. His mind raced with possibilities, imagining these invisible giants scattered across the universe, silently influencing the fabric of space and time. This revelation, he thought, could revolutionize humanity's understanding of the cosmos.

The very next day, Michell meticulously drafted a paper detailing his groundbreaking idea. He described how a star of sufficient mass and density could trap its own light, rendering it invisible. With a sense of exhilaration, he sent his work to the Royal Society of London, hoping to spark a revolution in the scientific community.

Though Michell's theory was published, it failed to ignite the fervor he had envisioned. The concept was too abstract, too ahead of its time for a society still grappling with the scale and nature of the universe. Michell's vision of dark stars faded into obscurity, a whisper lost amid the clamor of more tangible discoveries.

Nearly a century later, Albert Einstein and Karl Schwarzschild introduced the theory of General Relativity, reviving Michell's idea under a new name: black holes. These enigmatic entities, direct descendants of Michell's dark stars, captured the imagination of scientists and the public alike, forever altering humanity's understanding of space and time.

Michell passed away in 1793, his ideas largely forgotten by his contemporaries. Yet, his legacy endured, a testament to his unyielding curiosity and courage to question the boundaries of knowledge. His work, though overshadowed in his lifetime, became a cornerstone of modern astrophysics.

While the passage of time may have eroded his name from the annals of common knowledge, Michell's spirit lives on in every question asked and every boundary pushed. His dream of looking beyond the visible, of seeking answers in the unknown, remains a guiding light—a legacy that will persist as long as humanity continues to gaze at the stars.

CHAPTER SEVEN

Truth Buried Alive

About the Author: Avani Gujrati
I was born in 2008 in Varanasi, where I have lived my whole life. My mother is a homemaker, and my father is a businessman. The stories and rich culture associated with this city often inspire my own creations. Since childhood, I have loved reading thrillers and mysteries, with Sometimes I Lie being one of my favorite books. I aspire to become a lawyer, but if given the chance, I would love to pursue a career as a writer.

****

I'll be honest. I didn't really 'plan' on killing her. It just sort of...happened. She was just there, and well, I did it. Let me tell you something. I'm not the type of man who goes around killing people. I'm a very respectable person in my community. People like me; they trust me; they come to me with their problems... But well, you don't come this far without making a few enemies. It wasn't about anger. It wasn't even about her. She was just in the wrong place at the wrong time. One minute, she was standing there, accusing me of all sorts of things, and the next, well, I guess she was gone. I'll admit, though, something was building inside me for a while. When you live your life a certain way—when people look up to you and depend on you—you learn to keep control. You learn to push things down and to manage expectations, both theirs and your own. But that night... that night, something broke. Every day you wake up, you go about your day, thinking everything's normal and nothing could make this day out of the ordinary. And then, out of nowhere, something—or someone—throws everything off course. It started innocently enough. My day had been long and frustrating, like it usually is. I'd just come back from a council meeting—another pointless session with people squabbling over nonsense. As usual, they looked to me for leadership and for decisions. But no matter what I said or did, it wasn't enough. It never was. There was always someone unhappy, someone waiting to undermine me. That's the price of success, I suppose. You become the person everyone leans on, but eventually, someone starts pulling at the foundation. She wasn't one of those people, though. She wasn't a threat. Not really. But she thought she was, and that's where the problem started. Her name was Daisy. Such a pretty name. It's a shame she had to die like this. I'd known her for years. She was smart and resourceful, always sticking her nose where it didn't belong. She worked at the town paper, doing these local interest pieces—highlighting businesses and interviewing residents. Nothing serious. But recently, she'd been digging into things she had no business knowing about. My business. At first, I dismissed it. People like her—they like to feel important. They like to stir the pot and make people talk. But it wasn't until she showed up at my office, unannounced, that I realized how far she was willing to go. I remember the way she barged in that evening, her eyes bright, filled with something like triumph. She'd uncovered something, or so she thought. Something about the new development on the outskirts of town, about zoning permits and money that didn't quite add up. She accused me of cutting corners and of bribing the right people. She was right, of course, but she couldn't prove it. And I couldn't let her. She sat across from me, leaning forward in her chair, so full of confidence. "I know what you've been doing," she said. "And I'm going to expose it." I could have handled it differently. I could have told her she was wrong, laughed it off, and made her feel like a fool for even thinking I'd do something like that. But I didn't. I couldn't. Not that night. There was something about the way she looked at me—like she'd already won—that made my skin crawl. I stood up, trying to hide the rage that was fuelling inside my body behind a nasty smirk. "Oh really? And what exactly, may I ask, is it that you're going to 'expose' me to doing?" I asked her. She didn't back down. "Well then, let me tell you", she said, her voice dripping with self-righteousness. "You've been using your position to make yourself rich while this town suffers. People are losing their homes, and you're getting a cut of every deal." It wasn't true—well, not completely. Sure, I'd benefited from the deals. Who wouldn't? But I hadn't hurt anyone. I wasn't the villain she wanted me to be. I was just... taking advantage of opportunities. The way any smart person would. But she didn't see it that way. She kept pushing, kept talking, and with every word, the walls I'd built around myself started to crack. My reputation, my standing in the community, my whole life—I'd worked too hard to let someone like her tear it all down. "I'm giving you a chance," she said, standing up now, her voice sharp. "You can come clean, or I'll take what I have to the paper. People will listen, and they'll believe me. This whole town will turn against you." And that's when I snapped. I don't remember grabbing her.

I don't remember anything. All I know is that one minute we were arguing, and the next, my hands were around her throat. I squeezed, not thinking about it. I just wanted her to stop talking, to stop looking at me like I was nothing. She tried to fight back, her nails scratching at my hands, her eyes wide with shock and fear. But I didn't let go. I couldn't. Not until it was over. Not until she stopped moving. When I finally let go, she crumpled to the floor, her body limp and her face pale. I stood there for what felt like hours, staring at her. The reality of what I'd done didn't hit me right away. I didn't feel guilt or panic. Not then. I just felt calm. But that calm didn't last. I kneeled beside her, checking for a pulse, though I knew it was pointless. Her skin was cold, her lips blue. She was gone. Dead. And I had killed her.

I should have called the police. I should have turned myself in. But instead, I sat back in my chair, breathing heavily, trying to think. I couldn't let anyone find out. Not about her, not about what she knew. My entire life would be ruined. All my hard work would go down the drain, just because of some stupid girl. So, I cleaned up. I dragged her body to the trunk of my car, careful not to leave any trace behind. I drove to the outskirts of town, where the new development was still under construction. It was late, and no one was around. The foundation for one of the new buildings had been poured, but the concrete hadn't been fully set yet. I dumped her there, under the wet cement, and watched as the grey sludge slowly swallowed her up. No one would find her. No one would know. They didn't need to. I drove back home, washed my hands, and went to bed. I slept like a baby that night. For weeks, no one noticed she was gone. People just assumed she'd left town and moved on to a bigger story. Her colleagues at the paper didn't think much of it. But eventually, people started asking questions.

The police got involved. They searched, but they found nothing. They won't. And now, here I am, sitting across from you, telling you all this. Why? I'm not sure. Maybe I just needed to say it out loud. Maybe I'm tired of carrying it around. Or maybe I'm just testing you. Seeing if you'll believe me. You see, people trust me. They always have. And even if anyone wanted to do something about this, they wouldn't. Because there's no evidence. There's no proof. Just my word, and who's going to believe a story like this? After all, I'm a respectable man in my community. And people like me.

CHAPTER EIGHT

The Guardian of The Realms

About the Author: Avisarika Singh

I was born on March 18, 2008. My father is a scientist, and my mother is a homemaker. I lived in Arunachal Pradesh until I was 10, after which we moved to Varanasi. While I wouldn't consider myself a bookworm, I have a passion for fiction, especially Indian mythology, as it stretches the imagination to new heights. Movies are also one of my favorite pastimes. Writing is an unexplored skill for me, but I thoroughly enjoyed crafting this story.

*****

Karunyaa is a 17-year-old brown girl with long luscious curls, bright brown eyes, and a radiant smile. She grew up in a loving family, surrounded by luxury and comfort. She loved dressing up in vibrant clothes, adorning herself with jewellery, and dancing to the rhythm of classical music. Her life was beautiful, woven with love, laughter, and joy until the day she lost her parents in a tragic accident.

With a heavy heart, she travelled to the mystical town of Kalindrashetra from the bustling city of Calcutta in the 17th century, accompanied by her loyal servant's daughter, Kishori, who was the same age as Karunyaa.

Kalindrashetra, surrounded by the Aravalli Hills, was her ancestral place where the rest of her relatives lived; her parents moved to Calcutta because of their business. The valley was full of secrets and legends, rumoured to have some connection to the ancient epic, the Mahabharata. As she travelled through the winding paths. She felt a connection to this land, as if the hills held the secrets, which only she could unlock.

Karunyaa stepped into Kalindrashetra, and the town was completely different from what she imagined it to be. The town's vibrant atmosphere enveloped her. The streets were full of life, filled with laughter and music in the air. Karunya settled into her ancestral home, surrounded by her loving family. Her aunt and uncle, Rajeshwari and Raja, welcomed her with open arms, while her cousins, Dev and Radhika, bombarded her with questions. As they shared stories of their ancestors, Karunyaa felt a deep connection to her heritage.

While exploring the town with her cousins, she noticed temples containing some sort of symbol, and then she quickly saw her wrist; the same symbol was present, which was a birthmark according to what her parents told her. The marketplaces were filled with artisans and merchants, and ancient festivals were still celebrated. However, the whispers of mystery continue in the town—the strange glowing light in the night sky, the symbol she saw in the temples. Karunyaa sensed that beneath Kalindrashetra's joyous surface lay hidden secrets.

One evening, while exploring the ancestral home, Karunyaa stumbled upon an ancient diary. The diary belonged to her grandmother, Kalyani Devi. As she flipped through the pages, she discovered the same symbol she saw in the temples and her wrist. She also saw messages referencing the Mahabharata, sketches of the Aravalli hills, highlighting hidden caves, a map, and some sort of code language with meaning.

Karunyaa shared her findings with Kishori. "Kishori, do you think this diary holds secrets about our family's past?" Karunyaa asked. Kishori's expression turned serious. "I've heard rumours, Karunyaa. Rumours about your family's connection to the Mahabharata."

That night Karunyaa could not sleep; her thoughts were full of the mysteries and the unusual things she witnessed in the town. She kept the diary with her. The symbol on her wrist glowed brightly.

Karunyaa was not yet overcome by her parents' deaths; she remembered them each day, and although her aunt and uncle were sweet, she could not share everything with them. So, she decided not to ask them about the diary.

The next day she woke up and decided to uncover the truth about the diary and the rumours about her family connection to the Mahabharata. Karunyaa slipped out of her room, diary in her hand, and made her way to the ancestral library. The library was filled with ancient texts, manuscripts, and scrolls.

She searched for any mention of the symbol she saw everywhere in the temples, including her wrist. Instead, she found a text in the Mahabharata that she never heard of; Kalindrashetra was mentioned in the text but with a different name, 'Alaknanda' meaning the hidden place. She knew that Alaknanda referred to Kalindrashetra because she used to hear stories from her grandmother about the Legends of Alaknanda, and her grandmother always gave a hint about Kalindrashetra being Alaknanda, but Karunyaa always thought of it as her grandmother's imagination and never believed them truly.

The text further continued, "Five elements, five temples, five scriptures to unlock, the secrets of Kalindrashetra, and the mysteries to rock."

Karunyaa realized that the text referred to the five temples in Kalindrashetra, each dedicated to one of the five elements: *Prithvi (Earth), Jal (Water), Agni (Fire), Vayu (Air), and Akash (Aether)*. She remembered seeing the temples during her explorations with her cousins.

She decided to confide in Kishori, who had been by her side since childhood. "Kishori, I need your help; I want to explore the temples in the town. Can you help me with this?". Kishori's eyes widened, but she nodded. "I'm always with you, Karunyaa. But we must be careful." Karunyaa nodded in agreement. Together, they made a plan to sneak out of the ancestral home under the guise of a morning walk.

They first navigated to the Vayu Mandir, which was located on a hill. In each of the temples was a hidden compartment, and the way to those was written in the book she found in her home. They both made their way to the compartment, and there was the same symbol present as on Karunyaa's wrist. Both the symbols glowed brightly, and then Karunyaa placed her wrist on the door, and the stone door creaked open. There was a parchment in the middle of the compartment. The scripture was etched on a feather-light parchment. Karunya took the scripture and left the compartment.

Next, they visited Jal Mandir, which was situated in the middle of the lake. There she entered the compartment, and the scripture was inscribed on a crystal.

Their journey continued at the Prithvi Mandir, built in a cave. The scripture was carved into a stone piece.

As the sun began to set, they visited the Agni Mandir, where they found the fourth scripture, which was written on a metal sheet.

Lastly, under the starry night, they visited the Akash mandir situated at the hilltop, and the scripture was etched on a dark parchment.

With all five scriptures in hand, Karunyaa and Kishori returned to the ancestral home. They carefully transcribed the scriptures into the diary, and the coded messages began to reveal their secrets. The diary now read:

"Descend into the heart of Aravalli,

Where ancient ones sleep and secrets dwell.

Follow the stream of the ancient river,

To the caverns hidden, where truth does deliver."

Karunyaa was filled with hope, and she was ready to explore the Aravalli Hills. Kishori's expression turned serious. "We'll need help. The hills can be dangerous; we are still new here."

Karunyaa nodded. "I'll ask Dev and Radhika to join us; I'm sure they will help us."

The group started their adventure before dawn. Karunyaa navigated the group through the winding paths, following the stream of the ancient river and the map in the book. Suddenly, Kishori interrupted. "Do you hear that?". A low rumble echoed through the hills. "Thunderstorm," Dev said. Radhika's eyes widened. "But there's no cloud in the sky." Karunyaa's instincts screamed caution. "Let's find shelter." A massive rock rolled down the hill, blocking their path.

The group somehow managed to get out from there, continuing their quest.

As night passed, they reached the entrance to the hidden cave.

An inscription greeted them:

"Only those who face their shadows may pass."

Karunyaa hesitated. What did the inscription mean? Kishori's voice whispered. "I think it's a test, Karunyaa."As they stepped into the cave, the darkness seemed to swallow them. Suddenly, visions of Karunyaa's past emerged:

Her parents' accident. Her ancestors' secrets. Her destiny.

Karunyaa confronted her fears, and the shadows receded. A hidden door opens, revealing an ancient chamber. Inside, Karunyaa discovered:

A mysterious artifact with an ancient text, a revelation about her true identity. "Karunyaa, you're..." Dev whispered. Karunyaa's eyes widened. "I'm what?"

Radhika's voice trembled. "You're the chosen one, and our family is of Kauravas descent."

Karunyaa was shaken.

The artifact, a glowing crystal, radiates powerful energy. Kishori's eyes sparkled. "This crystal holds the essence of the Kauravas." Radhika's voice whispered. "And the power to unlock the secrets of Kalindrashetra."

Suddenly, the chamber filled with an ethereal glow. A vision of Vasudeva Krishna like a form of energy appeared before Karunyaa. "Karunyaa, daughter of the Kauravas, you have been chosen to restore balance to the realms." Karunyaa could not understand the happenings, and being the chosen one, she was confused and had so many questions that hesitantly she asked, "But I? Why me?"

The energy answered, "Your grandmother was also the guardian of the realm, and so are you. The symbol on your hand is the Kauravas' mark, and the guardians of the realm only have this mark. Your family was given the responsibility for the protection of the realm, and now the responsibility falls on you. Follow the map. Gather the elements. Restore the chakra." Karunyaa's heart swelled with determination. "I accept the challenge," she said. Krishna's energy blessed her. The vision vanished and a sacred scroll appeared, leaving Karunyaa with more questions. What realms needed balancing? What challenges lay ahead?

Karunyaa unrolled the scroll, a map of the realms, a list of ancient elements, and a prophecy.

The prophecy read, "Five trials. Five choices. The fate of the realms."

"I'll face the trials," she said. As they exited the chamber, Karunyaa noticed a subtle change within herself. A newfound connection to the natural world. Dev's eyes widened. "Karunyaa, your eyes... they're glowing." Radhika's voice trembled. "With an inner light, you're awakening to your true potential."

Karunyaa set off, accompanied by her cousins and Kishori. Their journey took them to:

The Realm of Earth: Restoring the tree's vitality

Karunyaa stood before a lifeless tree surrounded by barren land. Karunyaa's first trial was to restore the tree's vitality. Closing her eyes, Karunyaa meditated, connecting with the earth's energy. Kishori, Dev, and Radhika stood by her side, offering silent support. As Karunyaa visualized roots growing deep and leaves sprouting, green shoots burst forth, reviving the tree. The air filled with the scent of blooming flowers, and the earth's energy pulsed through Karunyaa, acknowledging her success. Trial one: passed.

The Realm of Water: Trial of Empathy

There was a hidden temple submerged beneath the ocean. The ocean had high tides that clashed against the rocky coastline. Karunyaa dove into the ocean's depths, navigating currents. Dev, with his knowledge of the ocean's rhythms, guided her through the water currents. Radhika's intuition helped them avoid deadly sea creatures. As they approached the hidden temple, guarded by majestic sea creatures, Karunyaa conveyed a message of harmony and respect to the beings by using her powers, allowing them to enter the temple. Inside, the Pearl of Empathy glowed. Karunyaa's hand closed around the pearl, and its strength spread through her veins. Trial two: passed.

The Realm of Fire: Trial of Courage

Flames engulfed the landscape ferociously. Dev's bravery inspired Karunyaa as she stood firm with courage. Karunyaa raised her hands, and a soothing melody calmed the blaze. Kishori's gentle voice harmonized with Karunyaa's, creating a calming effect. The flames danced, responding to their combined efforts. Trial three: passed.

The Realm of Air: Trial of Awareness

Karunyaa navigated the wind maze, guided by Radhika's intuition. Kishori's sharp instincts detected hidden patterns. The maze's center revealed a glowing feather, symbolizing awareness. Trial four: passed.

The Realm of Aether: Trial of Unity

Karunyaa and her group confronted the trial of unity. Obstacles came into their path, testing their cohesion. United, they overcame each challenge, their bond strengthening. The crystal of Unity awaited them, radiant with an otherworldly glow. Karunyaa's group grasped the crystal, their unity forged in the heart of the realm. Trial five: passed.

With all trials completed, Karunyaa returned to Kalindrashetra's cave. The Chakra's restoration began as she inserted the elements:

Earth's vitality

Water's empathy

Fire's courage

Air's awareness

Aether's unity

The chakra glowed, radiating balance. The realms were now safe, their harmony restored.

The same energy appeared and said, "Well done, Karunyaa. You've restored balance. Your destiny is fulfilled."

Karunyaa smiled with pride and said, "My journey's just begun."

Karunyaa discovered her true purpose: guardian of the realm. Harnessing her Kauravastra, she acquired the power of the elements. Her powers grew, safeguarding the realm's balance. As the sun set over the Aravalli hills, Karunyaa watched, knowing her ancestors' legacy lived on through her. The secrets of Kalindrashetra remained safe, protected by the resilient warrior she had become.

Mystery of Bloodied Heads

About the Author: Ayush Khandelwal
I am a 17 years old young and ardent writer who loves to read and write stories though this is my first one and I deeply hope that it will resonate with you. Writing stories for me is a journey of exploration, where thoughts, emotions and imagination fuse together to form a divine combination, called a story. Every word of my story carries a glimpse of my deep imagination. I look forward to hearing your thoughts and reactions in anticipation.

*****

The night hung heavy with an eerie, palpable tension as if darkness himself watched in hushed anticipation. The old, crumbling house on the outskirts of New York loomed in the fog, its decaying facade barely visible through the mist. Inside, sprawled across the cold floor, lay the world-class detective and fighter, once synonymous with justice, now reduced to a broken, blood-soaked shell. His body, a testament to strength and resilience, now betrayed him at his every attempt to move, each motion, a searing reminder of his crushed state. Some might have believed this to be a suicide mission for which he had been hired, but the truth was far darker. This was not a mission but a personal vendetta, born of the agent's deep, unrelenting grudge. The grudge that had festered ever since he failed to solve the most brutal and haunting crime he had ever encountered in his career.

Allow me to introduce the detective who has become a legend in his own right. His code name was Richard Brown—a name known to few, and even fewer knew his real identity, for he guarded that secret fiercely, even from the most important documentation. The reason behind his anonymity remained a mystery of its own. His early life was far from simple. In his childhood, he was often considered a withdrawn and quiet child, labelled as "dumb" by his peers and community. But, in truth, he was anything but a nincompoop. His quietude was a mask for his sharp, observant mind, which never ceased to observe, catalogue, and analyse every detail of the world around him.

As he grew older, his keen ability to notice the smallest details honed him into one of the world's most formidable agents. His career as a detective was inevitable, shaped by the very skill that had once made him an unsocial being. His physical presence matched his intellect. With a muscular physique and intense yet captivating eyes on a chiselled face, Richard held a demeanour that exuded both strength and focus. But his belief in his prowess, his unshakable confidence in solving any mystery, would soon be put to the test in ways he had never anticipated.

The morning of September 27th, 2005, had left an indelible mark on his life. That day was unlike any other for New York City. The unthinkable happened—the city's commissioner and his entire family, including their bodyguards, were found brutally murdered in their beds.

No threat calls. No traces of an intruder. It was a crime so shocking, so chilling, that it shattered the peace of the city and had set the stage for a mystery, unlike anything Richard Brown had ever faced.

The entire city was gripped by an overwhelming sense of terror and sorrow, the brutality of the murders leaving a permanent scar on its heart. The commissioner's mansion was immediately sealed off, and a red alert was issued across New York City, as the residents waited in dread for answers. In response to the chilling crime, the mayor appointed Richard Brown to lead the investigation. His arrival was met with a wave of relief by the people, who now held onto the faint hope that justice, security, and clarity would follow.

But as Richard entered the crime scene, even his seasoned mind faltered at the appalling sight before him. The massacre was unlike anything he had ever encountered. The commissioner's house had become a gruesome tableau of death. Ten people had been slaughtered—each decapitated, their heads placed around their bodies in a grotesque circle. The headless corpses were bound together, drenched in blood. The heads were placed on the floor, arranged in a perfect circle, with blood slowly pooling beneath them. It was a sight so horrendous that most would have fainted or at least been overcome by nausea. Yet, Richard stood unmoved by the scene—he had seen horrors before, though this one was particularly chilling.

Without wasting a moment, he began his investigation. His sharp eyes scanned the room methodically, his mind already racing through possibilities. But as he and the forensic team examined every inch of the space, they were met with an unsettling realization that there was not a single trace of the killer. No fingerprints, no footprints, not a single piece of evidence to track down the doer of such a heinous act. Richard meticulously searched the room, his practiced gaze sweeping over every object, every corner. Yet, despite his thoroughness, the room yielded nothing. The silence of the scene was deafening, and the mystery deepened with each passing moment.

A close look at the seance circle of the bloodied heads, Richard, finally caught a detail he had missed before, from the mouths of one of the severed heads something was protruding. His curiosity piqued, Richard leaned in closer, and he discovered a folded piece of paper hidden in between the teeth. It was as if the killer had anticipated Richard's every move, knowing he would find it. He stood frozen for a moment, stunned by the killer's intelligence.

With a swift motion, Richard extracted the note and unfolded the blood-soaked note. The message sent icy chills down his spine: *"I am inside one of your belongings and you know where to find me."* The words were stark, and Richard's instincts told him that this note had been left specifically for him. The killer knew he would be the one to investigate the case. But how? Richard's mind began to race—what did the note mean? What did the killer mean by "inside one of your belongings"? Richard didn't waste a second. His gut told him he had to leave the crime scene immediately. He was no longer just investigating a murder; this was a game, and he was now the target. Leaving behind a room full of puzzled officers, Richard made his way back to his own home, the weight of the words in the note pressing heavily on his mind.

Upon arriving at his house, he went straight into overdrive. Richard turned his place upside down, frantically searching through his belongings. Every drawer, every cupboard, every object he could think of. His mind, sharp as ever, was ticking like a clock, but every lead seemed to be a dead end. After hours of exhausting effort, he collapsed into a chair, physically and mentally spent. He sat there, staring blankly ahead when his hand instinctively reached into his coat pocket for his phone

It was then he realized that he hadn't checked his phone since the morning yet. He pulled it out, opened the message section, and scrolled through his messages, hoping for some clue, some piece of evidence that might connect to the note. And there it was. Among the many unread messages, one stood out—a message from an unknown number. Richard's pulse quickened as he opened it, his eyes scanning the screen for what he hoped would be the breakthrough he so desperately needed.

The message was sent to Richard from an unknown number, and at the exact moment he had discovered the note in his head, a shiver ran through him. It confirmed what he had feared—the killer was watching him, following his every move, and had somehow known that he would be called to solve this case. The realization that the killer was not only cunning but also tracking his every step left Richard momentarily paralyzed. His instincts screamed that this wasn't just a twisted murder mystery, it was a personal vendetta, one that was being played with him as the prime victim.

He opened the text message, his eyes scanning the words with growing unease: *"The chiming of the clock at midnight will signify my presence but make sure that you are not mistaken. Find me if you can Mr. Brown"*. For a brief moment, Richard entertained the thought that the killer might be a mentally disturbed individual, someone obsessed with the childhood games of treasure hunts or puzzles. But as the words sank in, he quickly dismissed that theory. This wasn't a game—it was something far more sinister.

Richard felt a wave of frustration wash over him. This wasn't going to be an easy case to crack. The killer wasn't just hiding in plain sight; he was carefully orchestrating his every move, toying with Richard's mind like a puppeteer. This was going to be one of the most complicated and dangerous cases of Richard's career—a test of both his intellect and his resolve. Richard sank into his chair again, still trying to make sense of the note. His mind, overworked and frazzled, eventually gave way to exhaustion, and he passed out into a deep, dreamless sleep.

When he woke up the next morning, the sunlight streaming through his window was the first indication of how much time had passed. He glanced at the clock, his eyes widening in horror—he had overslept and it was already late in the morning. Panic surged through him as he rushed to freshen up but his neck protested with a cramp due to sleeping in an uncomfortable position on the chair.

Had the killer already acted upon his threat last night? Was the deed accomplished while he had slept, unaware? With these thoughts, in a frenzy, Richard threw on his usual attire—black trousers, a crisp white shirt, and his signature brown coat. The final touch was his trusty Fedora hat, which, when placed on his head, transformed him into the experienced, relentless detective he had come to be known as. With no time to lose, he hurried to prepare himself for whatever awaited him next, knowing that every second mattered.

Richard breathed a sigh of relief when he visited his journalist friend and found that no further murders had taken place overnight in New York City. It was a temporary sense of calm, but he knew better than to let his guard down. The killer's threat was clear, and he feared the worst would come in by the next midnight. The game was far from over, and Richard needed to act swiftly. Without wasting another moment, Richard called upon the journalist to accompany him to the mayor's residence. Time was ticking, and the stakes were growing higher with each passing second. Once at the mayor's office, Richard requested an emergency meeting with all the city's top officials and higher authorities. The gravity of the situation required their immediate attention.

As soon as everyone had gathered in the chamber, Richard launched into a detailed account of the horrific murder he had encountered, the cryptic messages he had received from the killer, and his mounting concerns. The room fell eerily silent, as the weight of Richard's words heavily breathed on everyone's neck. The tension in the air was palpable, as the revelation of a killer who could evade all traces and leave behind such a bloodcurdling message struck a nerve in everyone present. The silence seemed to stretch on indefinitely, with no one brave enough to break it.

Richard was the first to, break the silence by rising from his seat. He addressed the room, his voice steady but urgent. He outlined his problem: the killer had taunted him with messages, but Richard was still unable to decipher the exact location where the next murder would occur. The cryptic line about the "ringing of the bells at midnight" was all they had to go on, and it wasn't enough. As he looked around at the sea of pale-faced officials, Richard could see the uncertainty in their eyes. They were just as perplexed, terrified, and desperate for answers as Richard himself was. Richard knew he couldn't solve this alone. The city depended on him, and they needed to work together to track down the killer before his next move.

Richard's mind raced as he processed the events unfolding before him. There, standing near the clock tower with a few officers in uniform scattered all over the place only Richard alone was standing under the street lamp near the tower. The plan had been set. Everyone, including Richard, would arrive at the clock tower by 11 PM. The goal was clear: to catch the killer and end his reign of terror. The air was thick with tension as they waited for midnight, the moment when the killer had promised to appear as the clock chimed.

As the clock struck midnight, however, nothing happened. No eerie chimes echoed through the air—just the chilling silence that hung over the gathering. Richard's pulse quickened, and an unsettling feeling began to settle in his gut. Fifteen minutes passed, then twenty, and still, no one in sight. He knew like him others too were waiting with bated breath for a single moment of action. Richard stood motionless, his eyes fixed on the towering structure, trying to make sense of the situation. He had been so certain. So certain that the clock tower was the key to solving the puzzle.

But then it hit him like a bolt of lightning. He had been deceived, not by the killer, but by his assumptions. The killer's words had played him. Richard had fixated on the clock tower, but there was another possibility he had overlooked. He had been so focused on the clock chiming at midnight that he had ignored a vital detail. A memory flashed through his mind, and his heart skipped a beat. There was an old man in the city, a reclusive figure known for his obsession with clocks. The old man had installed two large, antique clocks in his house, placed carefully in a specific room. The bells rang periodically, much to the old man's delight. It was a small, eccentric detail, but one that Richard had somehow neglected amidst the frenzy of the investigation. Richard's eyes widened in realization. The killer knew that Richard would overthink the clues, and in doing so, he made Richard believe that the clock tower was the true location. In reality, it was the old man's house, where the clocks chimed periodically alerting the neighbourhood about the time. That held the key. The killer had likely planned to carry out his sinister work there, knowing that Richard would focus on the clock tower.

With renewed determination and trepidation at its peak, Richard quickly turned to the group of officers and said, "It's not the clock tower. It's the old man's house. The clocks... they chime there, and that's where we need to go." The officers, though startled by the revelation, quickly rallied to action. It was a race against time. Richard knew that if they didn't act fast, the killer would slip away once again. The night was still young, but the killer's deadly game was far from over.

Richard's mind was a whirlpool of frustration and determination as he stopped with a screech in front of the old man's house. He had barely breathed a word to anyone before he dashed out, knowing that every second counted. The eerie chime of the clocks grew louder with each step he took, and a cold sweat drenched his brow. He could hear the sound of the pendulum reverberating in the distance, each chime driving him closer to the horrific truth.

When Richard finally arrived, breathless and panting, the sight that greeted him chilled his bones. The old man, whose obsession with bells had drawn Richard's attention in the first place, was lying lifeless on the floor. His body was pale, the blood drained from him in an unmistakable sign of brutal murder. But that wasn't what set Richard's blood on fire. Sitting casually on the windowsill, as if waiting for an audience, was the killer. His calm demeanour, and his nonchalant pose, made Richard's rage flare like wildfire.

Richard didn't hesitate. His anger and desperation pushed him forward, and he charged toward the killer with every ounce of strength he had left. But the killer, ever the elusive mastermind, had already anticipated this move. In one swift motion, he climbed out of the window and bolted in the opposite direction, disappearing into the night. Exhausted from the already frantic pursuit, Richard struggled to keep up. His legs were heavy, his breath ragged, but he pushed on, knowing that he couldn't let the killer slip through his fingers. He could hear other officers also catching up with their cars. He ran with the killer's shadow trailing just out of reach, each step seemingly pulling him farther from the city he had sworn to protect.

The chase led him through winding alleyways and unfamiliar streets until he stumbled upon an old, decrepit house at the end of a forgotten road. The air around it was thick with decay, and something about the place screamed danger. Richard's instincts flared as he cautiously approached, his hand on the grip of his gun. This was no ordinary house—it looked as though it hadn't been touched in years, perhaps decades. Inside, the stench was overwhelming. The place reeked of death and rot. As Richard ventured further, he nearly tripped over the lifeless bodies scattered across the floor. The stench of the blood that spread across the floorboards, painting a gruesome picture of the killer's twisted sanctum made him feel nauseated. It was clear now that this was where the killer felt at home—among the carnage, the blood, the macabre. This was where his madness had festered.

Richard's heart pounded in his chest as he moved forward, his senses alert for any sign amid the eerie stillness. Then, a faint sound of laughter hit his ears. It was devilish gradually escalating, and it seemed to come from all directions. It echoed off the walls, bouncing through the house like a thousand voices daunting him. Richard's pulse quickened, his head spinning with confusion. He couldn't pinpoint the exact source of the sound. It felt like it was closing in on him from all angles, a sinister symphony designed to break his resolve. The laughter was maddening, and it became harder for Richard to focus on anything else. He could feel his grip on reality starting to slip. Was it the killer? Or was it just his mind playing tricks on him? Determined to be undeterred Richard pressed on his motive of finding the source of the sound. He had come too far to turn back now.

Just as he was about to push a door open, a sharp, searing pain piercing through his chest spun Richard's world into darkness. His legs gave way beneath him, and he crumpled to the floor in a heap, unable to see if the killer was lurking anywhere in the shadows. His vision blurred, as the weight of the pain made it hard to keep his eyes open. He tried to push himself up, but his body refused to cooperate, a burning sensation spreading from his chest to his limbs. Before he could find the strength to rise, a vicious blow to the back of his head sent him spiralling into unconsciousness. The sound of the metal rod striking his skull echoed through his dazed mind, and darkness claimed him as his blood pooled on the ground, mixing with the dust of the decaying house.

The hospital corridor fell into a heavy silence as Richard's family and friends stood anxious to learn about his condition. His condition had deteriorated so dramatically in the past few days, and now, it was something they could never have prepared for. The doctors had just informed them of the shocking news: the bullet, which had narrowly missed Richard's heart, had lodged itself in a dangerous position within his heart. Miraculously, it hadn't caused the catastrophic damage they had feared. The bullet had passed through the superior vena cava and became embedded in the apex of his right ventricle. It was a medical anomaly that left even the most seasoned surgeons baffled.

It wasn't until three days later that Richard finally regained consciousness. The exhaustion and pain from the injury had left their mark on him, but his body had managed to survive, as it always did. His eyes fluttered open, and for a brief moment, he simply stared up at the white ceiling above him, disoriented. When his family and the officials walked into the room, a flicker of recognition passed through his gaze—but it quickly faded.

"Richard, my son, how are you feeling now?" his mother asked, her voice trembling with concern.

He blinked, his brows furrowing as if trying to piece together the fragments of his identity, but his mind was blank. The familiar faces surrounded him, the room filled with those who had been his closest allies—none of them seemed to matter to him at this moment. His mind was a blank slate. He could not recognize any of them. He didn't even know his name. The mayor stood silently at the back of the room; his expression sombre. Everyone had hoped for Richard's recovery, but no one had anticipated this outcome. The once brilliant detective, the man whose mind had been sharper than any blade, had lost the very thing that made him who he was, his memory.

"Richard?" The mayor spoke softly, stepping closer to the bed. "You were our best hope. You solved the toughest cases... You were the one who could have stopped him."

But Richard just stared at him, unblinking. There was no recognition in his eyes, only confusion. His mind, once so quick and sharp, was now clouded by a profound and inexplicable amnesia.

"I'm sorry, but I don't know who you are. I don't even know who I am," Richard whispered, his voice a fragile echo of the man he once was.

The weight of his words hung heavily in the hospital room. The silence was deafening, filled with the knowledge that they had lost more than just a detective. They had lost the person who could see the truth when no one else could, the person who had solved mysteries with a mind that operated at a level above all others. Now, that person was gone, replaced by a man who didn't even know his past.

As they stood there, witnessing Richard's pitiable condition it became clear that the case was far from over. The killer, whose presence had haunted Richard's every move, was still out there while Richard, now unable to recall the events that had led to his near-death, was no longer in a position to bring a justified end to the case. The world around him had changed in an instant, and it was unclear if the detective would ever regain the memories or the resolve that had once made him so formidable.

The doctor's stern voice echoed through the tense atmosphere. "There is only one way to bring his memories back," he said, his gaze fixed on Richard, who was staring in confusion at the bed. We must take him to the place where he was attacked after he had healed. After a week, Richard was taken to the killer's sanctum again accompanied by all the people he knew including the doctor whose presence was very crucial. As they all started to get close to their destination, Richard's face had a confused yet familiar look as if he had recognized something but the look faded again. The crowd reached the killer's sanctum and so did Richard. Richard just stood there and gazed at the old and horrifying house. Suddenly Richard dropped to the ground on his knees. His hands clutched his head tightly as if trying to hold onto something, anything, to stop the torment that racked his mind. Richard's screams were desperate, filled with confusion and anguish. His body trembled as though the very essence of his identity was being ripped away from him, piece by piece. The others stood frozen, unsure of what to do. His family, friends, and the officials could only watch in horror as Richard, once so strong and capable, now seemed utterly broken.

For a few agonizing moments, no one spoke. The only sound that filled the air was Richard's painful cries. Then, just as suddenly as it had begun, the pain stopped. Richard fell silent. His body remained motionless on the ground, and his eyes slowly opened, glazed but sharp. His breathing was heavy, but he no longer screamed.

"Richard," the mayor called cautiously, kneeling beside him. "Can you hear me?"

Richard blinked, his gaze distant, as though trying to gather the fragments of his past. His face was pale, covered in sweat from the agony he had just endured. Slowly, he tried to push himself up, using the ground as leverage. His movements were sluggish, but he was regaining some semblance of control over his body.

"I... I remember something," he murmured, his voice shaky but clear. "It's all coming back... slowly."

The mayor and others exchanged glances; their hearts filled with hope. The doctor stepped forward, his eyes scanning Richard's face, looking for any sign that he was truly returning to himself. "Tell us what you remember," the doctor said, his tone patient but filled with anticipation. Richard took a deep breath, his hands still trembling as he sat up, supported by the mayor and the doctor. He looked around, his gaze settling on the decrepit house,

"I remember... the killer. I remember chasing him." Richard's voice was steadier now, and as he spoke, fragments of the case started to piece together in his mind. "I remember the notes, the murder... the heads... the clock tower... the clocks chiming."

His voice faltered for a moment as he gazed at the decaying house. "This place... it was here. This is where everything started. The killer knew I was coming. He played with me, made me chase him... and now I understand."

The group leaned in, their eyes wide with anticipation. "What do you understand, Richard?" the mayor asked quietly. Richard stood up slowly, his legs still weak but steadying. "This house... it's not just a sanctuary for the killer," he whispered, almost to himself. "It's a trap. I was never meant to find him here. This place is his hiding place, but it's also the place where he planned to destroy me—psychologically, not just physically."

He paused, his eyes scanning the surroundings. "I've been through hell to get here. The killer isn't just hiding. He's waiting. He wanted me to get lost in my mind, to chase shadows until I lost who I was. But... I won't let that happen."

The mayor's face softened with a sense of relief, but the doctor remained cautious. "You're certain, Richard? You're not just grasping at straws?”

Richard nodded firmly, his eyes locking onto the doctor's with renewed strength. “I know now. The killer is still out there. He's not finished with me, not yet. But I'll finish this. I won't let him win”. The group stood in silence, absorbing Richard's words. Despite the immense toll the case had taken on him, it was clear that the fire inside him hadn't been extinguished. The killer had made one fatal mistake—he had underestimated Richard Brown. Now, with his memory returning, Richard was more determined than ever to end the madness that had almost consumed him. Two days later when another anonymous message came, Richard was prepared to take the chance again. According to the message, the killer wanted Richard to meet him at Liberty Island. The killer wanted him alone and Richard made up his mind to satisfy the killer's sinful desire.

The others, however, weren't as resolute. They stood around him, their faces filled with concern, worry, and fear. The mayor, the doctor, and even Richard's mother tried to convince him to stay put and wait for backup. “You can't go alone, Richard,” the mayor pleaded, his voice resounding with concern. “This killer has proven time and again that he's dangerous. We need a proper plan.”

But Richard, his jaw set in a firm line, shook his head. “No. I have to do this singlehandedly. The killer wants to play games, and I'm not going to let him keep controlling this case. I'm going to Liberty Island to end it, and no one is going to stop me.”

The mayor grabbed his arm, his grip firm. “Richard, think about it. You've already been through hell. You're not thinking clearly. You don't know what you're walking into.”

Richard wrenched his arm free, looking the mayor squarely in the eyes. "I've thought about it more than you know. The only thing left is for me to face him. I can't keep running away. This ends tonight."

With a final, resolute glance at everyone, Richard turned and left. His steps were determined, unwavering. His mind was made up, and nothing could change it. The others hesitated for a moment, exchanging looks of helplessness, but they knew there was no stopping him now. Richard had always been a man of action, and once he set his mind to something, there was no turning back. The boat ride to Liberty Island was tense. The night air was cold and crisp, biting on the skin. Richard stood at the edge of the boat, staring ahead, his mind focused on the mystery that had consumed him. He thought of the voice on the recording, how it had taunted him with the promise of answers. As he approached the island, Richard felt his heart pounding in his chest He could almost feel the killer's presence looming over him, waiting in the shadows. He was close, too close.

The boat docked at the island's shore and Richard alighted with a sense of purpose, his instincts sharp, his senses on high alert. As he made his way towards the island, the air seemed to grow heavier, as if the very ground beneath him held secrets. The silence was oppressive, broken only by the sound of his footsteps and the distant rush of water. Richard had no idea what awaited him, but he knew it would be the final confrontation. He reached an old, abandoned building in the middle of the island. Its structure was decayed, the windows shattered, and the door barely hanging on its hinges. The building was barely visible under the moonlight but Richard pushed the door open, stepping inside without hesitation. Inside, the room was dark, save for a faint sunlight coming from a shattered window. Richard stepped forward, his heart racing. Then, from the shadows, the killer emerged. The man who had tormented Richard for so long finally revealed himself—his face was twisted with a sick grin, his eyes gleaming with madness.

"Ah, Mr. Brown," the killer's voice was smooth, almost mocking. "I knew you would come. I knew you couldn't resist."

Richard's grip tightened on the gun in his hand, his finger hovering over the trigger. "This ends here, today.," he said, his voice cold and steady. The killer chuckled. "Oh, Richard, you don't even know that you've been playing my game all along. But now, it's time for the final piece to fall into place."

With a sudden movement, the killer lunged forward, and Richard's world was rocked by that destructive blow by the killer on his head with a heavy metal. Richard's body felt like it was breaking with every movement. Blood trickled from his bruised face, and his vision was blurry, but he refused to let it show. The pain was unbearable, but his determination to stop the killer was stronger than ever. He could hear the killer's laughter echoing through the darkness, taunting him.

"Is this it, Richard? Is this the best you've got?" the killer mocked, his voice dripping with malice. "I've been playing with you from the start. You're nothing but a pawn in my game."

But Richard's mind was sharp, even if his body was failing him. Through the haze of pain, he could hear the killer's tone which made him realize the truth. The killer wasn't just a maniac; he was a master manipulator. Richard wasn't just fighting for survival—he was fighting against someone who had been pulling the strings all along;

someone who had planned this entire game. With a growl of determination, Richard wiped the blood from his eyes and steadied himself. His legs wobbled, and his breathing was ragged, but he wasn't done yet.

"You think you've won?" Richard rasped, barely able to hold his stance. "You've underestimated me. You won't get away with this."

He knew he was running on pure willpower now, his body a vessel for the anger and resolve that filled his heart. The killer stood in front of him, grinning, still confident in his dominance. Richard couldn't afford to make another mistake. He needed to outsmart him, outmanoeuvre him. The killer lunged again; a blow aimed at Richard's head. In that split second, Richard saw an opening. With whatever energy he had left, he dodged the punch, grabbing the killer's arm and twisting it in a swift, calculated motion. The killer staggered slightly, surprised by Richard's sudden strength.

This was Richard's chance. He fought through the pain, using his body's momentum to push the killer against the cold stone wall. For the first time, Richard saw a flicker of doubt in the killer's eyes. He wasn't invincible after all. Richard's hands locked around the killer's throat, his grip tightening with all the fury and exhaustion he had left.

"You're done," Richard snarled through gritted teeth. "This ends now."

But before Richard could deliver the final blow, the killer let out a chilling laugh. "You think you've won? You still don't understand, do you?"

Richard hesitated, just for a moment, and in that instant, the killer broke free from his grip with unnatural strength. The killer pushed Richard away, sending him crashing to the ground, the pain shooting through him like fire.

"You're just a part of the plan, Richard. You always have been," the killer said, his voice now a low, menacing growl. "Do you think I wanted to kill you? You were never my target. The game is bigger than you."

Richard's heart skipped a beat as the realization hit him with a jolt. The killer wasn't after him—he had been after something else all along, something far more dangerous. Richard wasn't the true victim. He was merely a player in a much darker, more complex game. Suddenly, everything clicked into place. The strange messages, the cryptic notes, the twists and turns of the case—they were all part of something bigger, something far more sinister. Richard's eyes burned with renewed focus. His mind raced as he pieced the puzzle together in his head. "Then what was the plan? What do you want?"

The killer's smile widened, revealing the satisfaction in his twisted game. "You'll never know," he sneered. "But you'll be the one to finish it. You'll be the one to carry it out". Richard's pulse quickened as he understood the killer's words. It was always about the endgame, and he had just been handed the most crucial piece of the puzzle. But Richard was no longer just a pawn. He was ready to take control of the situation.

With a final surge of adrenaline, Richard stood tall once more, ready to confront the killer with everything he had left. The island, the darkness, the twisted labyrinth—it was all coming to an end. And no matter what, Richard knew one thing for certain: he was going to make sure the killer's game ended that night. All at once, another devastating blow from the killer to his head, brought Richard back from his thoughts to the present only to engulf his mind into darkness with the lethal blow. The killer seeing the opportunity, tried to gain victory over Richard but this time Richard blocked his punch by grasping the killer's fist tightly. The killer was stunned at Richard's strength after consuming such deadly blows. Seeing the surprise in the killer's eyes, Richard started punching the killer's face almost shattering his jaw. Then with a metal clothesline that he found on one end of the room, Richard turned the killer upside down and he collapsed on the floor. Richard dropped to his knees to unmask the killer and ultimately end the mystery. With trembling hands, Richard sent the killer's mask flying in the air. As he saw the face of the killer, Richard crawled on the ground on his hands backward in horror as if he had seen the devil's face. It was him, Richard's dearest friend Victor who was dead for the whole world. Richard was heartbroken because of two reasons. One was that his dearest friend was trying to kill him and the second was that he won this fight but in an unwanted manner. Richard was completely exhausted and his face was covered in tears as he did not want to continue this anymore. Richard sat there on the floor gazing at Victor's face. It was a painful revelation, but Richard pushed past the shock, focusing on the present moment. He couldn't afford to dwell on the past now. The truth was staring him in the face: Victor had been manipulated for sure, twisted into a tool for something much darker. And now, he was part of something bigger, something more sinister than Richard could have ever imagined.

Just then Victor regained consciousness to see Richard crying. Seeing his moment, Victor grabbed a small hammer from his pocket and hit it hard on Richard's head. Now it was Richard who was unconscious. Without wasting a moment, Victor hauled Richard into his captivity. After a couple of hours, Richard woke up from his senseless state to find himself in a dark room. Fighting with the fogginess in his head, he saw a shadow emerging from the darkness and it was none other than Victor. "Why?" Richard managed to rasp; his voice hoarse. "What do you want, Victor? What's the end game?"

Victor's eyes narrowed as he stopped pacing. "You don't get it, do you? It's not about what I want. It's about what they want. They've given me everything—power, control, knowledge. All I had to do was follow their orders". Richard felt a shiver of dread crawling up his spine. "Who are 'they'?" he demanded, his pulse quickening. Victor smirked. "You think this is all just some random chaos? This is part of a much larger plan. The pieces are in place, Richard. You were never meant to stop me. You were just a distraction. And now, you'll be a part of their grand design."

Richard's stomach twisted as the implications of Victor's words sank in. Whoever "they" were, they had orchestrated everything from the start. The murders, the manipulation—it was all part of a much larger puzzle, a game where Richard and Victor were merely pawns. And now, Richard was tangled in something far more dangerous than he had imagined.

"You think you can control me?" Richard spat, his voice growing stronger despite the pain. "You think you can use me like you've used everyone else?"

Victor's eyes flickered with something—regret, perhaps, or guilt—but it was quickly masked by his usual cold demeanour. "I don't have a choice," he said, his voice low and dangerous. "You never had a choice either. You're in this, Richard. Whether you like it or not."

With every word Victor spoke, Richard felt his resolve harden. He couldn't let this end like this. He couldn't let Victor win, even if it meant facing the terrifying unknown that loomed ahead. Richard had been through too much to back down now. Victor stepped closer, his hand resting on a control panel on the wall. "You'll see soon enough. You'll be a part of the plan whether you help me or not."

Richard's mind was racing. There had to be a way out of this. His hands were bound, but his mind was still sharp. He remembered the adrenaline syringe from before, the rush of energy that had kept him going when he was on the brink of death. It was a long shot, but maybe there was something similar around here, something to give him the edge he needed. With a deep breath, Richard shifted his body, testing the chains that held him in place. He had to get free. He had to stop Victor and whatever larger conspiracy was at play. With every ounce of strength he had left, Richard pulled at the chains, using every muscle in his body. It was slow, agonizing work, but he felt the chains loosening, one by one.

Victor turned his back momentarily to Richard as he checked something on the control panel. It was now or never. With a final, desperate wrench, Richard broke free from his restraints, landing hard on the floor. He didn't waste a second. He lunged at Victor, knocking him to the ground, the shock of the sudden movement catching him off guard. The two struggled, the air thick with tension and rage. Victor fought back, but Richard was fuelled by something stronger now—a need to end this, to stop the game once and for all. With a surge of energy, Richard overpowered Victor, pinning him to the floor.

"You don't get to win," Richard whispered through gritted teeth. "Not today."

He looked around the room, searching for something, anything, that could help him bring this nightmare to an end. The control panel, the mysterious symbols on the walls—it all pointed to something bigger. Something that he still didn't fully understand. But right now, stopping Victor was all that mattered. Unexpectedly, in a flash, a bullet hit Victor's leg out of nowhere.

Victor staggered back, his face contorting in pain as the bullets hit his calves. He stumbled to the ground, his body unable to bear the weight of the injury. His breathing became ragged, and blood started to pool around him, staining the floor beneath him. The room was filled with an eerie silence, broken only by Victor's pained gasps.

Richard stood over him, his expression cold and resolute. Richard had no clue where the bullet came from, and his face was pale, expressionless Swiftly, a man came out of the dark and stood behind Richard. Richard felt footsteps behind his back and he was too scared and burned out of new twists in the game, but he turned around and met the man's gaze. Again, Richard was stunned and this time it was a big one as there stood a bitter enemy from his past, Tom. Without saying a word, Tom came so near Richard that they could feel each other's breath and shook his hands as if signing a pact. Richard understood the whole situation. He started to believe the fact that Tom was there to forget the past and help Richard in this.

Tom stood beside Richard. Despite their tumultuous history, Tom had changed. They were no longer enemies, and Richard knew that together, they could stop Victor and whatever plans he had set in motion.

Victor looked up at them, his eyes filled with a mixture of hatred and disbelief. "You think you can stop me?" he spat; his voice weak but laced with venom. "You think this is over?", Richard's voice was steady, but there was a dangerous edge to it. "It's over for you, Victor. You've played your part in someone else's game. But it ends now."

Victor's lips curled into a twisted smile, even as blood dripped from his wounds. "You're naive, Richard. You have no idea what you've just walked into. This isn't just about me. There are forces—bigger than you, bigger than both of us—that will ensure this goes on, whether I'm here or not."

Richard felt a chill run down his spine. Despite Victor's condition, his words were chilling. It was as if he was speaking from a place of knowledge as if he was warning them about something far more dangerous than they could imagine.

Tom stepped forward; his tone more forceful than Richard's. "Who's behind this, Victor? Who's pulling the strings?"

Victor's smile faded, replaced by an almost sorrowful look. He gritted his teeth, clearly fighting to stay conscious. "You still don't get it, do you?" he murmured, his voice barely above a whisper. "There are people who never wanted you to solve this case, Richard. People who needed you out of the way... and now, they'll finish what I started."

Richard's mind raced as he processed Victor's words. There was something deeper, something darker at play. He had suspected for a while that Victor's actions weren't his own, that he had been manipulated—brainwashed, even—but this? This was something far more dangerous.

Soon, Victor collapsed on the ground with a loud thud due to a great loss of blood. Richard called the police from Tom's phone, and they arrived in about 20 minutes. They all flew from Liberty Island to New York in the army's helicopters. Upon reaching New York City, Victor was immediately taken to the hospital, and Richard and Tom went to their places after exchanging their numbers. Victor was again healthy in a few days, but still, he was vulnerable, so he was taken to jail and thrown in the maximum-security zone. New York City was now quiet and everyone's lives returned to normal, including Richard's. He took a holiday to spend some days from the hustle of his detective life. But deep down in his heart, Richard knew that the real villain was still to be found. There were no clues, and Victor's interrogation was completely useless. So, Richard had to give up for some time and wait for the real villain of the story to appear and once again make his life a nightmare.

As the days passed, Richard tried to settle back into a semblance of normal life. He spent his days trying to unwind, indulging in the peace he had longed for after the chaos that had surrounded him for weeks. He took time off from his usual work, allowing himself to relax and reflect. But deep down, a nagging feeling lingered in his mind. Victor's cryptic final words echoed, reminding Richard that the true mastermind, the one pulling the strings, was still out there. The feeling of unfinished business gnawed his heart time and again leaving him restless despite the calm on the surface.

Meanwhile, Tom remained in contact with Richard, though both of them kept their distance from the investigation. They knew the danger of pushing too far, of stirring up something that wasn't ready to be uncovered. But they also knew that the real enemy was still at large and that their time to act would come soon enough.

Months passed, and life in New York gradually returned to its normal pace. People resumed their routines, the city regained its usual energy, and the streets were once again filled with bustling crowds. Yet Richard couldn't escape the haunting feeling that the quiet was only temporary.

As the shadows of the city stretched long, Richard knew one thing for sure: the real game would soon begin, and he must be prepared because anything could be kept in store for him. This time, he wouldn't be caught off guard.

CHAPTER TEN

The Lost Voice

About the Author: Ayush Kumar

Born in Bihar , Ayush Kumar is looking to be the next big thing in literature at the young age of 17. Currently pursuing his education at Sunbeam Bhagwanpur , Ayush is on the lookout for his big break with this compelling short story .

*****

Even though a week had passed, Jacob could not get the voice out of his head. He had been hearing it all week after that call, and although it was only in his dreams, he knew something was off. It was stuck inside his head, refusing to leave. He went to bed frustrated, but not enough to prevent him from sleeping. The next thing he felt was a voice that kept calling out to him, saying his name. It sounded as if it were a cry, a desperate call for help, but simultaneously a kind and calming whisper. The voice was daunting yet soothing. It was the same one he heard a week ago. The voice, it seemed like, was getting louder by the minute, and Jacob felt like whoever was calling for him was getting closer. He could sense that the voice was now right in front of him. For a moment, he thought he recognized the voice, but before he knew it, Jacob woke up.

It was an average Tuesday morning. Jacob, still slightly dazed, realized that he had things that needed to be done. He got out of bed, got ready, and asked his dad for a ride to school. It had been almost an hour since he had woken up, but still, he was wondering whose voice it was that he heard. On their way to school, Jacob's dad tried to make conversation, but instead of answering in complete sentences, Jacob awkwardly nodded and made sounds of affirmation to everything his father asked him about. He was too invested in his mysterious dream to care about small talk. They made it to school; Jacob exited the car and wished his dad goodbye. He looked a little embarrassed while doing it, as he had to do it in front of his friends, but the embarrassment didn't last too long. He slowly made his way to the front gate while saying hello to a few acquaintances. He entered the halls a few minutes later, and there he met Elliot, his classmate. Jacob was not surprised to see Elliot because somehow they'd always find each other before class started. They talked a bit while moving toward their classroom. Even though several hours had passed, the strange dream and the unknown voice were still somewhere in the back of Jacob's mind, but he carried on with the rest of his day as he normally would.

The time went by particularly quickly for Jacob that day. Maybe it was because he had a lot on his mind or perhaps because he had two history classes, and before he knew it, school was almost over. Only 5 minutes remained until the last bell would ring, and everyone started packing up by then. Jacob did so as well, and while putting his books inside his bag, he glanced at the class door and saw a bunch of students walking past the halls, and among them was Charles, a friend he hadn't talked to in a while. Jacob wanted to say hello to Charles, but he realized he couldn't because he knew it would take the teacher a couple more minutes to dismiss the class. When the class was finally dismissed, he hurried into the halls looking for Charles, but after looking for a while and not finding him, he decided that he'd talk to him some other day and headed for the exit as he knew that his father would be waiting to pick him up. While he was walking down the hall, he heard it.

"Jacob....?"

The world went silent. Everyone around him disappeared. Jacob stood there, stunned. His heart was pounding, but his mind went completely numb.

"That's it," Jacob murmured.

The voice matched perfectly. Everything that had happened to him rushed back into his mind. The mysterious phone call he received a week ago. The anonymous caller said nothing except his name. The strange dreams he was having were someone calling out to him. Could it be them? Jacob wanted to turn around and see who it was, but he felt like he didn't have the strength to do it. He felt as if death itself was behind him, and if he looked at it in its eyes, he would succumb to it. But still, using all the courage that he had, he turned around. As he did, the world felt like it was turning back to normal. He could slowly feel people around him and hear the noises being made. This panoramic feeling of gaining senses was almost relieving to a degree. And then, when he fully turned around, he saw it. The person who had been on his mind for so long drove him insane. The person he could not stop thinking about, who would not leave him alone, even in his dreams. The person who he wasn't expecting to be someone from his school. The voice was... Charles?

"Surely not," Jacob exclaimed.

A look of horror was seen on Jacob's face. A look that Charles noticed. Charles didn't expect Jacob to look so weary upon seeing him, especially since they hadn't talked in a while. To Charles, Jacob looked like he was almost disgusted to see him. Charles wondered for a moment if Jacob looked so distraught on seeing his way because of his shaggy hair or because they hadn't talked in so long that Jacob was upset with him. But seeing that look on Jacob's face made Charles a little worried. He had never seen Jacob like that. So, without thinking any further, Charles approached Jacob.

'Hey, are you alright?'

Jacob looked at Charles for a while before saying anything. He was still in disbelief. He thought to himself, "Could it be Charles? This whole time?". He was so utterly confused by this situation that he couldn't think of anything to say. He questioned whether he should talk to Charles about everything that was on his mind, but he decided not to.

"Yeah. I'm alright," Jacob muttered.

Jacob left without saying anything else. He immediately went where his dad would park and got inside the car without saying anything. Jacob's dad wanted to ask why Jacob seemed so cranky but decided not to, as he thought it was probably because he had a bad day and it would be best to leave him be. The car ride home was completely silent; not a word was shared. The entire time, Jacob was confused but also frustrated. He couldn't understand why he would have those dreams over Charles and why he, of all people, was the one calling out to him. To him, it didn't make any sense. Charles was an old friend. They were in the same class a couple of years ago. He and Charles got along well too. But as time went on, they slowly grew apart.

They talked less, hung out together less, and at one point, they stopped seeing each other because they were simply too busy. He thought all of this while started going through his phone and checking who that strange call was from, though he did the same thing the day he received it. He matched it with Charles' number, but it wasn't the same.

The second he got back home; he went straight to his room. He wanted to call Charles and ask him whether it was he who called Jacob a week ago with a different number, but he hesitated. He stared at the call button on his phone, questioning whether he should press it. He did, regretting his choice for a moment, but then Charles answered shortly after. Jacob started by apologizing for the way he acted in school when he saw Charles. Charles asked if Jacob was feeling well; Jacob said yes, and he explained that the reason he acted that way was because he was having a pretty bad day. They talked a little more, and before hanging up, Jacob asked Charles if he had called him a week before. Charles said that he didn't, Jacob went silent for a while, briefly said his goodbyes, and hung up the call. Jacob realized that it wasn't Charles who was the voice. But during the call, Jacob noticed something else. At school, talking to Charles was so much different than talking to him now. At home, talking to Charles felt relieving, but at school, he felt like he got transported to a different place. But something felt off. Jacob felt a little strange every time Charles said his name. He noticed that in his dreams, the voice would also just say his name, and when he first heard Charles in school, what made him feel so uneasy was Charles saying his name. But it wasn't just that. A lot of people had said his name throughout the day, but that didn't trigger anything. Then, an idea struck Jacob. Jacob had moved a lot in the past, so he had to change schools quite frequently. This meant that he had a lot of friends who were very close that Jacob had lost contact with. He thought of this because Charles was also a very close friend of Jacob; he was the first friend he made when he joined his current school. And like all previous friends that he had, he drifted away from him.

Jacob started reminiscing. He started thinking of the first school he went to when he was just a little boy. He sifted through all the musty memories and remembered how much fun he had as a kid at that school. He could almost feel the old playground, the slide, and the hanging bars, which felt like they were a mountain to climb. He remembered that there was someone else playing with him, some other boy. The boy who became his first friend. Though Jacob was having trouble remembering what he looked like, a name was loudly ringing in the back of his mind.

Jacob looked through his phone again to look for the unknown number. This time he decided to call it, though he already did the day he received the call. But now he was prepared. He pressed the button and waited. Though he was ready now, a little byte of anxiety was loading into his body for every second that the call wasn't answered. Jacob thought that the ringing would go on for all of eternity, but at last, it ended. Jacob figured that this was probably the end and he wouldn't be able to contact his lost friend, but then it struck him. Since they were friends, their moms would probably know each other. That meant they probably had exchanged contacts. Upon realizing this, Jacob headed straight towards his mom and asked her for her phone. His mom got scared for a second because she couldn't think of any reason why Jacob would want her phone so urgently that he'd run straight toward her at full speed like a maniac. His mom handed him the phone, and Jacob grabbed it as fast as he could. He headed towards the lawn while tying in his friend's name. The contact showed up. His heart started beating at a speed he didn't think it could. He stared at it for a whole minute. He didn't know what was going to happen if he called that number, but he knew that he had to do it. His heart was pounding faster as his finger moved closer to the button, to the point when it felt like it would rip itself out of his chest. He pressed it, but the feeling didn't go away; the sound of the ring only added to it. Jacob thought his friend's mom would pick up the call, so he was further confused about what he would say. His hands were shaking, sweat was falling from his face, and he felt like he wouldn't be able to stand for much longer as he was trying to think what he would say. But suddenly... it stopped.

"Raymond?"

There was a long pause. A million thoughts entered Jacob's head. And then he heard it.

"Jacob?"

CHAPTER ELEVEN

Broken & Healed

About the Author: Bhavya Singh
I was born on December 29, 2008, in Varanasi. My father is a businessman, and my mother is a homemaker. I enjoy everything my mother cooks, but her tomato pasta is my absolute favorite. I am a big fan of anime, with Naruto being one of my favorites. My dream destination is Japan. I can be cheerful one moment and, in the blink of an eye, angry or upset, but overall, I tend to be a generally happy person.

*****

"I am getting late, Anya. I'll catch you later." The door slammed shut behind her. Poor Anya's eyes were filled with tears as she saw her mother get into the car and race into the traffic.

"Is it wrong to ask you for your time? Don't I have the right to spend some time with you, to tell you how much I love you, to hug you, and to rest my head in your lap?" Many such questions arose in Anya's mind. She wondered if she would ever get to spend some quality time with her mother.

Anya was fifteen. She had pearly black eyes and long brown hair that rippled like cascades of brown water. She was five when her father passed away. She had nobody else to call her own except her mother, Geetanjali, a tall and slender woman perfectly built to become an athlete. But of course, she did not choose to become one. Instead, Geetanjali joined politics to secure her daughter's future. She set up a political party in which people showed faith eventually.

She became so busy getting her party organized that she did not have time to spare for her daughter. In a corner of her mind, she had believed that Anya would forever be looked after if her mother was powerful in the system. But that reason somehow got lost along the way. Now Geetanjali was a popular public figure and had also become rich in no time. She wanted to move into a new house, built according to her wish. Geetanjali had become a materialistic woman. She spoke to a broker on the phone: "I need vacant land big enough for a huge bungalow. I'll bid you the best price if you get me the best land. What time can I meet you tomorrow?"

Anya overheard the conversation and asked her mother, "Are you going somewhere?"

"Oh yes, I am going to meet the broker tomorrow. We will take a look at a fine piece of land where I'll build a beautiful mansion. I cannot live any longer in this matchbox," replied Geetanjali.

"Why, mummy? You are thinking of leaving this house. I can feel Papa's presence here, in times of good or bad. This is where my childhood memories reside. I am not going to leave this house," said Anya angrily.

Her words expressed her firm belief. She was not going to budge from her decision. Geetanjali had no other option but to drop the whole idea. For a minute, she, too, was overwhelmed by a deluge of memories and her eyes pricked with unshed tears. She blinked them away; tears wouldn't take her anywhere.

"But you should not cling to the past so much that you can't move ahead," Geetanjali tried reasoning one last time.

"Why don't you understand that money is not everything? Anyway, I am going to sleep. Good night."

In the morning, Geetanjali was on the phone again. "Yes, Mr. Mishra, I will be reaching within 15 minutes," she said, walking to the car.

"Mom, I am ready," an excited Anya called after her.

"Oh, Anya, I forgot to tell you. There is a meeting with the party workers; it was arranged just now. It's urgent, so I will not be able to come with you."

"Mom, this is the fifth PTM you are missing. You know I'll get my report card today."

"I'm getting late. No time, Anya. I'll catch you later."

Anya went to school alone to collect her report card.

She got back home at noon, but her mother wasn't home yet. Her report card was really outstanding, and it had melted her anger away. She loved to cook when she was happy. She went straight to the kitchen to make backed cheese pasta. She garnished it with grated mozzarella cheese—just the way her mother loved it.

Her mother returned home but was in no mood to have dinner.

"But Mom. I haven't had anything since returning. I thought that we would have dinner together and then you would see my report card."

"Did I tell you that we'd have dinner together? Or that I have time to see your report card? Don't you realize how much work I have to do every day?"

"But why don't you realize that I need your time, Mom?" she said as she went sobbing to her room.

That night, Anya was very upset. She cried her heart out. She did not know what to do. But an idea struck her. She remembered how her grandmother always said, "Ganga is divine. She cleanses everybody's sins. She loves everyone." Anya thought that maybe she could find peace and solace there. Even though the Ganga was not her real mother, she could give her attention, at least. She decided that Ganga would become her companion.

The next day after school, she went to meet her new companion. She saw the divine water, the holy spirit of Ganga, numerous temples along the bank, and a glistening expanse. She was mesmerized. Her mind lost control, and her feet inched towards the river as if they were under a spell. She had visited the Ghats several times before, but never before had she felt such a powerful tug.

Earlier, she thought that Ganga was nothing but a victim of pollution, but now she could sense the ripples of water filled with love for the hundreds of pilgrims who came to her every day. She decided that she would spend her entire day being rowed in a boat, sketching, painting, and watching the sunset and showering its light onto the glistening water. Anya soon developed a bond with Ganga and its surroundings.

The neighbourhood children mocked her for it. "Her mother does not have time for her, so she spends her entire day outside," they would say, but Anya pays no heed to them.

On the other hand, the neighbourhood woman developed a liking for her. "Why do you go out? It's burning outside. Please stay inside dear. If you wish to go out, carry a bottle of water with you. You are so pretty. Don't lose it to the sun," they often said.

One day, Anya returned from school and found her mother at home. Perhaps she hadn't gone to work that day. Her mother called her out: "Anya, check if there is a painkiller lying on the table. Bring it to my room. I am not feeling well."

Anya handed the pill to her mother. She was about to leave when her mother said, "Take care," and gave her a beautiful smile. For Anya, it was the first time in her life since his father's death that she had seen her mother smiling. She felt heavy-hearted that day; her mother was unwell, and she was worried for her. She went to the riverbank and sketched a woman sitting in the temple and immersed in prayer. After finishing her sketch, she took a dip in the water and prayed for her mother.

When she returned she saw her mother shivering. At once she called the doctor, who told her that her mother had a fever and that she would recover in a day or two.

The next morning, Anya left for school, but Geetanjali took a pill and stayed at home to rest. But it was not to be; she was constantly disturbed by the cook, Mr. Mishra, and others. Some workers wanted a raise, others complained about their coworkers, and Mr. Mishra said he was being harassed by office staff for higher pay; otherwise, they would go on strike. Geetanjali did not get a minute of rest. As a result, her fever shot up considerably. Anya returned from school and felt her mother's forehead; it was burning.

"Mom, you must come with me to a place tomorrow. I want to take you there. I know you'll feel better," said Anya authoritatively.

Geetanjali agreed. The next morning, though she was drained and weak, her fever had abated, and she got ready to go with her daughter.

Anya took her mother to the Great River. She rented a boat, and off they rowed into the river. Geetanjali reclined against a cushion, watching the water and the sights of riverbanks. She was still not at her best. She hadn't been to the river in a long time. The last time was probably when her husband had passed away. She left herself lulled by the gently rocking boat, and tears flowed down her face. She wiped them and sat up wondering where her time had flown and where her life was.

Anya sat in front of her, looking at the waters ahead, her hair rippling down her back, and Geetanjali felt a sudden pang for her daughter. She reached out and touched her hair lovingly. She felt light hearted; her tears had washed away some of her many knots, and she would work on the rest.

Anya turned around: "You're fine now, Mum, thanks to Ganga. She took away your exhaustion in just 30 minutes. The doctor and medicines could not have done it even in days. Can you imagine how big her heart is?" Anya was indeed very happy.

"Thank you, my child. I am so glad you brought me here. I had forgotten the magic of the river, and you found it. It has changed me." She gathered Anya in her arms. "I did not care for the many tears you shed every day. Even then, you were concerned for my health. I am sorry. Please forgive your mom."

"Oh! Come on, mom. Who will take care of you if I don't?" She hugged her mother tight.

And just like that, their relationship was renewed. Geetanjali found her work-life balance again.

Anya grew up to be a famous painter. Her canvasses depicted the rich culture of Banaras. Each canvas had a handwritten note at the back explaining the significance of that particular place.

The note was written by none other than her mother.

Even today, you will find many people who come to the Ghats of Ganga just to heal their broken hearts and mend their relationships.

That's her magic, only hers.

CHAPTER TWELVE

To A Different Setting Beyond The Court

About the Author: Ishika Singh
I love watching anime and reading books as well as mangas. I'm also interested in sketching and drawing. I love exploring things that interests me a lot. I believe in 'smart work not hard work '.

*****

Yuno, a first-year at Tokyo High School, had always been passionate about badminton. Her mother, a good badminton player herself, died in an accident while traveling for a tournament. She loved her mother and wanted her passion to live on. That's one of the reasons why she wants to be the best.

Her bond with her mother cannot be expressed in words, as well as the pain she suffered when her mother passed away. She used to lock herself in a room and refuse to eat anything. Though when she realized how much her father was suffering but still working to give her a good life, she would come out and apologize to her father, who only felt relief that she came out.

Yuno joined the girl's badminton club as soon as she entered high school. She was liked by everyone because she was kind-hearted and helpful and got good grades in academics as well as sports.

The members of the girl's badminton team were kind, and the captain, Juvia, was really strong.

Although Juvia also had a hard life. Unlike Yuno, she didn't have a supportive parent. Her passion for badminton was being neglected; her parents, both business persons, believed that she should continue the family business when she grew up.

Despite being the best first-year player in the whole team, she was unable to beat the captain in a match. She even lost brutally to a score of 21-5.

For four months, she has been practicing for the inter high preliminary, which is a qualifier tournament that is held every year to determine which high school team will represent their prefecture in the spring high preliminary held for the whole country.

On 11ᵗʰ November, she starts practicing around ten o'clock at night. After an hour of practicing, she suddenly fell due to exhaustion and dizziness. She lifted her arm to look at the time, and it was 11:11 p.m. In the blink of an eye, the dark hall changed to a sunny day, and the raised arm provided shade to her eyes. She was confused, so she looked around, and while getting up on her feet, she found herself in a place that looked like a badminton court built many years ago.

Yuno saw familiar faces around her cheering someone's name. She looked in front and saw the captain of the badminton club and heard that Juvia won the match. Then she realized that she was defeated again, even without trying.

Her body was still sore from that continuous practice. After taking a few steps, she stumbled, but her mother caught her in the nick of time. She stared at her face. The last time she saw her face was seven years ago, when her mother had to leave for the tournament. Her mother took her to a house that seemed to be the place where she lived. Her mother made her sit on the bed and went and brought a first aid box. Her mother spotted a scratch on her elbow, so she started treating her wound, yet she said nothing.

Yuno thought that she was upset that she didn't win. She was about to apologize but was interrupted by her mother. She said, "I believe that you are trying your best, but you are unable to defeat Juvia."

Yuno replied, "I'm sorry."

Her mother said while interrupting her, "I think you forgot my words; let me repeat them for you. First, never forget the basics. Second, never apologize without a reason. Also, losing isn't a reason. Third and last, you ought to have self-belief."

Upon hearing those words, Yuno felt relief. She laid down on the bed, closed her eyes, and when she opened her eyes, she found herself back in the school court. She looked at the watch; it was 12th November, 05:37 a.m., and the practice started at 6:15 a.m.

Later at practice, she challenged the captain to a match. Juvia was about to deny it, but everyone wanted them to face off, so she eventually agreed to a match of 21 points.

Well, Yuno didn't win the match but she didn't lose brutally. She was only 3 points away from winning.

She pledged to remember her mother's words and surpass the captain before the tournament starts.

CHAPTER THIRTEEN

The Last Whisper of The Lotus

About the Author: Ishita Singh
Ishita Singh, was born in Kashi, the City of Light, in the year 2007.
She loves classical dance, music and arts.

*****

Part One: A Rising Tide

In the heart of the Mughal Empire during the late 17th century, the city of Agra thrummed with life. The majestic Taj Mahal rose against the horizon, a testament to love and loss. Among the bustling bazaars and fragrant spice markets lived Aditi, a young woman known for her vibrant spirit and sharp intellect. Her father, a skilled artisan, crafted intricate marble inlays, a trade that had thrived under the Mughals.

Aditi often accompanied her father to work, mesmerized by the beauty of the stones and the stories they could tell. She spent hours sketching designs, dreaming of one day creating her masterpieces. But the world outside was changing; whispers of dissent against Mughal rule echoed through the streets. The Marathas, led by the indomitable Shivaji, were rising, seeking to reclaim their lands from the imperial grip.

One day, while Aditi was at the market, she overheard a group of men discussing the latest skirmishes. "The Marathas will not rest until they reclaim their freedom," one man declared. "The Mughals may have the power, but the spirit of the people cannot be contained."

Aditi's heart raced at the thought. She had always felt the pulse of her land, and the idea of fighting for freedom ignited a fire within her. As the days turned into weeks, news of battles and brave warriors filled the air. Aditi felt a call to action, a longing to be part of something greater than herself.

Part Two: The Call to Arms

One evening, while her father worked on a commissioned piece for the emperor, Aditi made her way to a secret meeting of local revolutionaries. It was held in a dimly lit courtyard, where the flickering flames cast shadows on the walls. There, she met Arjun, a passionate leader known for his eloquence and unwavering commitment to the cause.

"Aditi," he greeted, his eyes sparkling with resolve. "Your father speaks highly of your talent. We need artisans like you to create symbols of our struggle—something to inspire our people."

"What do you mean?" she asked, intrigued.

"We're planning a resistance, and we need banners and weapons adorned with our history and spirit. Your designs could unify us," he replied.

Aditi felt a surge of determination. She joined their ranks, using her artistic skills to craft intricate symbols of hope. She worked tirelessly, often late into the night, her heart racing at the thought of what lay ahead.

As the Maratha forces grew bolder, news of their successes spread like wildfire. Aditi's resolve deepened, but so did the risks. The Mughal authorities were merciless, and any sign of dissent could lead to dire consequences.

One fateful night, as Aditi was leaving the meeting, she was ambushed by Mughal soldiers. Heart pounding, she managed to evade capture, but the encounter left her shaken. Fear and uncertainty danced within her, yet she knew she could not turn back.

Part Three: Flames of Rebellion

The next few months saw the tides of war shift dramatically. The Marathas, led by brave commanders, struck decisive blows against the Mughal forces. Aditi continued her work, now deeply embedded in the resistance. Her designs adorned weapons and banners, breathing life into their fight for freedom.

One evening, as she was unveiling a new design at a gathering, the atmosphere crackled with energy. Arjun stepped forward; his voice powerful. "This is not just art; it is a statement. With each stroke, we declare our right to our land and our people!"

The crowd erupted in applause, and Aditi felt a rush of pride. She was part of something larger—a movement that sought to reclaim their identity. But the weight of responsibility pressed heavily on her shoulders. She knew the stakes were high; failure could mean not only their demise but also the loss of their dreams.

As battles raged, the Mughals retaliated with increasing force. Aditi learned that her father had been arrested for his connections to the resistance. The news shattered her, fuelling her resolve to fight back. She decided to use her art as a means of communication, sending coded messages through her designs to inform fellow rebels.

One night, while working late, she was approached by a familiar face—Karan, her childhood friend who had enlisted with the Maratha forces. "Aditi, we're planning a major offensive. We need your designs to rally the troops," he said urgently.

"What about my father?" she asked, fear creeping into her voice.

"We'll do everything we can to free him. But we must act quickly; the time for waiting has passed," he replied, determination etched on his face.

Part Four: The Battle for Freedom

As dawn broke on a fateful day, Aditi stood with Karan and Arjun on the outskirts of Agra, the air thick with tension. They had united forces to take back the city, knowing that victory would change the course of their struggle. Aditi clutched the banner she had designed, its colours vibrant and bold, a symbol of hope for her people.

The battle erupted with a roar, swords clashing, and cries of valour ringing through the air. Aditi fought alongside her comrades, her heart pounding as she used every ounce of strength and skill. She could hear Karan's voice cutting through the chaos, rallying their forces.

Amid the turmoil, Aditi caught a glimpse of the Mughal soldiers, their armour gleaming in the sunlight. The realization struck her—these were not just faceless enemies; they were men, fathers, and brothers. But the weight of her purpose propelled her forward.

As the sun reached its zenith, the tide of battle began to shift. The Marathas pushed forward, fuelled by the spirit of freedom that coursed through their veins. Aditi, driven by the image of her father's face, pressed on, her resolve unyielding.

In the heat of the conflict, she saw Arjun fall, a grievous wound marking the end of his journey. A cry of anguish escaped her lips as she rushed to his side. "Stay with me, Arjun!" she pleaded, cradling his head in her arms.

"Aditi," he gasped, his voice fading. "You must carry on... for all of us. Let the lotus bloom."

Tears streamed down her face as she held him close. The weight of loss and grief threatened to consume her, but Arjun's words ignited a fire within her heart. She stood up, fuelled by his sacrifice, and raised the banner high.

Part Five: A New Dawn

As the sun began to set, the battle raged on, but the Marathas had gained the upper hand. The Mughal forces, overwhelmed and demoralized, began to retreat. Aditi felt a surge of hope, but the pain of loss weighed heavily on her heart.

With the city of Agra reclaimed, the people erupted in celebration. Aditi stood among them, her heart torn between joy and sorrow. They had won a crucial battle, but the war was far from over. Her father remained imprisoned, and the dream of freedom still hung in the balance.

In the weeks that followed, Aditi worked tirelessly alongside her fellow revolutionaries to establish a new order. They sought to rebuild, to honour the sacrifices made for their freedom. She organized efforts to rescue imprisoned artisans and provide support to families affected by the war.

One evening, while gathering with the remaining leaders, Aditi spoke passionately about the future. "We have fought for our land and our people, but we must also fight for our culture and our identity. Let us not forget the beauty of our heritage as we forge a new path."

Her words resonated with the group, and they pledged to ensure that the arts would flourish alongside their newfound freedom. Aditi's designs adorned the walls of the new assembly hall, each piece a reminder of their struggle and their resilience.

Epilogue: Legacy of the Lotus

Years passed, and the Maratha Empire grew stronger, establishing itself as a formidable power. Aditi became a celebrated figure, known not only for her artistry but for her unwavering spirit in the face of adversity. She continued to teach young artisans, instilling in them the importance of their craft and the power of art as a means of resistance.

In her heart, she carried the memory of Arjun and her father, their sacrifices a constant reminder of the struggle that had shaped her life. She would often wander the gardens of the Taj Mahal, a symbol of love that had inspired countless stories, reflecting on the intertwined fates of beauty and resilience.

Aditi understood that freedom was not just a destination but a journey—one that required continuous effort and dedication. She vowed to keep the flame of hope alive, ensuring that the whispers of the lotus, symbols of their struggle, would echo through the generations to come.

In the tapestry of history, her story became a testament to the power of art, the strength of community, and the unwavering spirit of those who dare to dream of a better world.

CHAPTER FOURTEEN

Hard To Be Me

About the Author: Kumari Prachi
Kumari Prachi is the eldest daughter of Mr. Keshav Kumar Baliyase and Mrs. Puja Baliyase. Growing up in a close-knit joint family, she fosters a deep respect for everyone around her. With a vivid imagination, Prachi loves creating her own imaginative stories that reflect her unique perspective on the world.

*****

It's hard. It really is. Hard to be me, hard to be a student. Only I know the sleepless nights, the sacrifices, and the relentless effort I poured into securing a 92% in my Class 10 board exams. The family functions I missed, the social connections I gave up even when I yearned to connect—everything was for a promise I made to myself: to gift my parents a result that would make them proud.

My parents are my world. They've always stood tall as the most important people in my life. I'm a carefree soul—unbothered by what others think of my style, my clothes, my accent, or anything else. The only thing I care about is my parents' happiness. Their smiles are my most treasured possession, and I can do *anything* to see them smile. By *anything,* I mean just that—*anything.* And so begins my story.

Scoring good marks in exams, however, isn't the ultimate success. Life is much more than that. To be truly successful, one must become financially stable and emotionally resilient. Without stability, without the strength to handle life's trials, marks are just numbers. I saw this stark reality when I moved to Kota for my Class 11 and 12 studies. Kota—a place synonymous with fierce competition, sleepless nights, and an obsession with marks, marks, and more marks.

Pursuing science, enrolling in Kota's coaching ecosystem, and preparing for the daunting JEE exams wasn't my dream. It was my parents' wish, and I didn't have the heart to go against it. Deep down, I always wanted to choose commerce, to delve into the world of business, to become a business tycoon. But fate, or perhaps my obedience, had other plans. I found myself in Kota, battling not only the academic pressure but also my inner turmoil.

Adjusting to life there was like stepping into a parallel universe. Fun, relaxation, and enjoyment were alien concepts. Nothing felt familiar. The city buzzed with energy, but it lacked warmth. With great difficulty, I tried to console my mind and settle into this new reality. Soon, the classes began, and I was thrust into a world where survival meant staying ahead of others in an endless rat race.

On my first day at the institute, I sat on the front bench, clutching my Physics book. The air was thick with tension as students murmured about the complexity of the syllabus. As the class started, someone came and sat beside me. I didn't bother to look up until this person greeted me warmly, breaking the silence. It was surprising—he was the first person in Kota to initiate a conversation with me. Everywhere else, I was the one who had to take the first step. That small exchange marked the beginning of our friendship—the only real friendship I had in that city.

Months passed, and the initial euphoria of adapting to Kota wore off. Mock tests began, and the pressure mounted. Having shifted from ICSE to CBSE, I found the first semester manageable and scored well. However, that success gave way to overconfidence. As the second semester began, my focus wavered. I procrastinated, lost sight of my goals, and indulged in distractions, such as attending cultural fests and watching late-night movies on my laptop.

My friend tried to pull me back on track, but I ignored his warnings, even snapping at him. While I slacked off, he gave his 100%. Yet, despite his efforts, he secured only 20% in the exams. My own performance wasn't much better—I scored 70%, a shocking blow to someone who had never dropped below 85%.

The aftermath of that result was a whirlwind of guilt and regret. I wanted to apologize to my friend for my behavior, but when I approached him, he seemed distant and heartbroken. I tried to console him, but my words fell flat. That night, I couldn't shake off the unease. Something about his demeanor felt final, like he had given up on something far greater than the exam.

The next day, a horrifying rumor circulated through the institute. "Did you hear? That boy who got 20%—he hung himself." The words hit me like a lightning bolt. Refusing to believe it, I rushed to confirm the news. It was true. My friend, my only friend, was gone.

I stood frozen, staring at his lifeless body, overwhelmed with guilt and despair. His mother's wails echoed through the room, and his father stood silently, hiding his sorrow behind a stoic face. The rituals that followed felt like a blur, but the pain was piercingly real. I lost not only a friend but also my peace, my joy, and a part of myself.

Depression engulfed me. I withdrew from everyone and everything. My grades plummeted further, and even though my parents tried to motivate me, their disappointment was palpable. The guilt of failing them weighed heavily on my shoulders. I spiraled into a dark abyss, battling anxiety, stress, and feelings of inadequacy.

At my lowest, I contemplated ending it all. The pressure was unbearable. But every time I thought of my parents, I couldn't go through with it. Their love was my anchor. It was their belief in me that kept me going, even when I felt like a shipwrecked soul in a stormy sea.

Eventually, I sought help. Yoga, meditation, and therapy became my lifelines. Slowly, I began to heal. One day, I encountered Rohan, an old friend from my hometown. He had always advised me against going to Kota, warning me of the relentless pressure. When I confided in him about everything—my friend's death, my depression, my struggles—he became my rock.

Rohan's unwavering support reignited my spirit. With his encouragement, I rebuilt myself piece by piece. My confidence returned, and so did my determination. I vowed not only to succeed for myself and my parents but also to honor my late friend and his family.

The preparation phase was grueling. I studied for 17+ hours a day, sacrificing sleep, food, and leisure. My focus was unshakeable—I had one goal: to qualify JEE Advanced.

When the results came, my hands trembled as I opened the website. And there it was—*PASS*. I had done it. Tears streamed down my face as my parents hugged me tightly. My success wasn't just mine—it belonged to everyone who had supported me, especially my friend's parents.

In that moment, I realized the power of resilience and the importance of mindset. Life in Kota had tested me in ways I never imagined, but it also shaped me into a stronger, more determined person.

I still think of my friend. To many, he might seem like a coward for ending his life, but I know he tried. He fought until he couldn't anymore. In my heart, he remains a shining star, a reminder of the fragility of life and the strength it takes to keep going.

It was hard—*so hard*—to be me. But I made it. And for that, I am forever grateful.

CHAPTER FIFTEEN

The Lavender Shadows

About the Author: Manasvi Srivastava

Born and raised in Varanasi, I'm Manasvi Srivastava. My name signifies intellectuality, mind control, and highness—seemingly contradictory concepts that keep me grounded and provide the perspective I need in life. What sets me apart is my relentless drive to push boundaries, whether I'm dancing, expressing myself through poetry, strumming my guitar on lazy afternoons, or aspiring to become a developer. With my story being published, I am thrilled to share my imagination and hope to leave a lasting impression while connecting with curious minds.

*****

The air was heavy and sticky last night as I left my windows wide open to catch any breeze. Around 2 a.m., a sudden crackling sound echoed from the nearby house—the very same house where that kind and giving old lady used to live. She was the sort of person whose presence could brighten even the cloudiest days for everyone in the neighborhood. Her warmth and kindness were an inherent part of her daily life, reflected in everything she did. Her smile was a constant source of comfort, and her kind words were a balm to everyone she encountered. Over the years, she treated me as if I were her own child, with a tenderness that deepened our bond to feel almost familial. Visiting her house was always a delight. The moment you stepped through the door, you were greeted by a subtle, soothing scent of lavender. It wasn't overpowering, just a gentle reminder of her presence, as if she were welcoming you even before you saw her.

She had an incredible way of making you feel instantly at home. As soon as you walked in, she would greet you with a warm smile and an embrace that seemed to melt away any worries. Her home always carried the scent of lavender, mingling with the aroma of freshly baked treats or whatever she was cooking. In the kitchen, a recipe book sat on the counter, its pages stained with splashes from countless meals. It felt like a secret history of all the dishes she had lovingly prepared, just waiting to be rediscovered. The staircase area often echoed with the sound of a vintage clock from the bedroom wall on the second floor—the kind with a pendulum that ticked softly in the background. The sound was oddly comforting, like a steady heartbeat in an otherwise quiet house. The entire place radiated an inviting atmosphere that made you feel truly cherished.

The day she died remains vivid in my mind. The circumstances surrounding her death were as shrouded in mystery as they were tragic—she was found murdered, and the case remains unresolved to this day. The cruelty of her demise seemed inexplicable for someone as gentle as she was. Her kindness was unparalleled, and she had no close family. Her late husband had passed away years earlier, and her children had moved abroad permanently, never to return. She was left alone with only her memories and a few distant relatives who were scarcely involved in her life, leaving no clear answers as to who could have done this or why. In the days leading up to her death, unsettling whispers spread among the neighbors. Some claimed they had seen her in the twilight hours, sitting by her window, gazing at old photographs, lost in a reverie of days long past. People remarked how, during those final days, her home seemed to take on a different, almost eerie atmosphere.

There was a peculiar stillness, as if the house itself had become aware of something ominous. Her eyes, usually so full of life, seemed distant and reflective, as though she were gazing beyond the present moment. Those who saw her during those final days described a strange calmness about her—a serene smile that felt out of place, as if she were quietly bidding farewell to a world she had deeply loved. It was hard to pinpoint what had changed, but there was an unspoken depth to her demeanor that left an indelible impression. She carried a tranquility that was both comforting and vaguely unsettling, like someone who had found peaceful acceptance of a truth they couldn't fully share.

When the police found her, the scene was both heart-wrenching and puzzling. The old lady lay on her living room floor, surrounded by family photos that seemed oddly out of place amidst the chaos. Her body bore dark, angry bruises—some large and swollen, others arranged in patterns that seemed almost deliberate rather than random. Her home, once a haven of warmth, now felt like the stage for a tragic finale. The faint scent of her favorite lavender still lingered in the air, interwoven with the metallic tang of blood, a haunting blend that seemed to echo her silent goodbyes to the family she had long since lost to distant shores. The brutality of her death was undeniable, yet strangely, nothing of value had been taken. No money, no jewelry—nothing was missing.

As the days turned into weeks and the investigation into her death dragged on with little progress, a chilling thought began to take root among those who had known her. Could it be that she had sensed her impending doom? Her calm demeanor in the days leading up to her death hinted at an unsettling premonition—a quiet acceptance of her fate. These questions lingered unanswered, as the truth about her final moments remained locked away in a silence that would forever be her own.

I was sent to my grandmother's house on the day of her final rituals to shield me from the trauma. It felt strange being away from the neighborhood during such a heavy time, but my family thought it was for the best. My grandma did everything she could to console and comfort me throughout my stay. We often had deep conversations that opened my mind to things I had never considered before. One thing she said has stayed with me ever since: "You know, there's something about a bright light that seems to draw all kinds of shadows. It's like when someone shines too brightly, they end up casting a long, dark shadow that follows them. It's as if the light itself attracts those who dwell in the dark, waiting for their chance to snuff it out."

When I finally returned home the day before, I was struck by a wave of unspoken grief. Hearing those crackling echoes from her empty house shook me, especially since she had been on my mind ever since I got back. I wanted to catch a glimpse of her house, but the windows were all boarded up, as if whatever was inside was too dreadful to witness. Slipping into my slippers, I made my way toward her house. The once-charming home now appeared abandoned and lifeless.

As I approached the door, it let out a creak that sent shivers down my spine. Despite the unsettling atmosphere, I pressed on, feeling a sense of unease I had never experienced in her home before. The once-welcoming scent of lavender still lingered, a bittersweet and haunting reminder of her absence and her final days. That's when it suddenly hit me—the clock. Why had it stopped ticking? Was it that, with her life ended, the clock had lost its purpose too? It felt so symbolic. But the absence of its usual rhythm created a suffocating stillness, as if the house itself were holding its breath.

I proceeded toward the staircase, each creak of the old, warped steps making me flinch. Yet, my determination to reach the bedroom on the second floor did not falter. The intense darkness around me felt almost alive, pressing in from all sides with every step, as though it were pulling me into a confusing, consuming void.

I could hear faint, echoing footsteps behind me, though no one was visible. Was it my mind playing tricks, or was there something far more sinister at play? Each step on the staircase felt like it could be my last. Suddenly, the oppressive stillness was shattered as two weathered hands, adorned with bangles, emerged from the shadows, reaching out toward me. The sensation was immediate and terrifying—a crushing grip around my throat, as though invisible fingers were tightening mercilessly.

I struggled desperately to free myself, but my voice failed me, too weak to call for help. With every ounce of strength I had, I managed to utter a single desperate cry, "Maa...!"

And then, just as abruptly as it began, everything shifted. The chaos dissolved, replaced by an inexplicable stillness. I found myself back in a strange, peaceful solace, as if those horrifying moments had never happened. I woke up to familiar surroundings—wrapped in my cozy blanket, lying on my comfortable bed. The grip around my throat was gone, and the suffocating darkness had receded, leaving me in an unexpected calm. Yet, I couldn't shake the lingering remnants of the dream, its vivid terror clinging to me like a shadow, refusing to fade.

"It was just a dream," I murmured, trying to reassure myself as I snuggled deeper into the warmth of my bed. But no matter how hard I tried to calm down, shivers continued to run through my body. Hoping to ease my racing thoughts, I made my way to the kitchen for a refreshing drink of water. The dimly lit room felt strangely unfamiliar as I reached for a glass and filled it with cool water, hoping it would steady my nerves.

Just then, I heard a faint rustle behind me. Startled, I turned to see my mother standing in the doorway. Her gaze pierced through me, a mix of concern and disbelief etched across her face. The tension in the air was palpable. She took a step back, her hand flying to her mouth in shock, her wide eyes brimming with terror. Her trembling voice broke the suffocating silence as she cried out, "What are those bruises and rashes around your neck, my child...?"

My heart stopped. Her words echoed in my ears as I instinctively looked down at my neck. The marks were still there, faintly throbbing, as if they had followed me out of the dream. My mother rushed toward me, her hands trembling as she reached out to touch the bruises.

The stinging sensation surged anew as her fingers brushed against the strange pattern on my skin. The marks weren't random—they seemed deliberate, almost symbolic, with a haunting resemblance to something I couldn't quite place. Her touch, though gentle, carried an unshakable chill that made the room seem colder with every passing second.

And then, an overwhelming realization hit me: her hands smelled faintly of lavender—so delicate, so sweet, yet so unmistakably familiar. A thought, unbidden and terrifying, flashed through my mind: had I unknowingly stepped into a story that was never meant to end?

Envy Eats Nothing But Its Own Heart

About the Author: Megha Singh

Megha Singh is a multifaceted writer and performer whose work intricately explores the tapestry of human emotions and the vastness of the cosmos. An avid astrophile, she draws inspiration from the stars, weaving cosmic themes into her narratives that delve into the depths of human connection and longing.

In addition to her literary pursuits, Megha is a trained Kathak dancer, a passion that significantly influences her storytelling style. With her unique blend of artistic intuition, she offers readers a profound and beautiful experience, inviting them to reflect on the complexities of life.

*****

In the bustling town of Varanasi, where the Ganges flows serenely alongside ancient temples, lived Aanya, a talented artist known for her vibrant paintings of the river and its people. Her art adorned the walls of galleries, attracting admirers and buyers from far and wide. But her success was not without consequence.

Her closest friend, Kavya, once a promising artist herself,

had seen her career falter in the shadow of Aanya's brilliance. The bright colours that filled Aanya's canvas only deepened the darkness in Kavya's heart. As Aanya thrived, Kavya found herself consumed by envy, a poison that seeped into her thoughts and actions.

Every evening, as Aanya painted by the riverside, Kavya would watch from a distance, her heart heavy. "Why her?" she would whisper to herself, a relentless cycle of self-pity and resentment spiralling within. Each compliment Aanya received felt like a dagger to her self-worth.

One day, driven by a desperate need to reclaim her place in the art world, Kavya made a fateful decision. She began to stalk Aanya, observing her every move, hoping to find inspiration or, more insidiously, a way to sabotage her friend's success. But instead of clarity, Kavya only found despair. The more she learned about Aanya's struggles and sacrifices, the more tangled her feelings became.

As weeks passed, Kavya's obsession grew. She started to mimic Aanya's style in secret, copying her techniques and ideas, hoping to rise again by leveraging her friend's talent. But her paintings felt hollow, lacking the soul that infused Aanya's work. Frustrated, Kavya's envy morphed into bitterness, culminating in a plan that could destroy everything.

During the annual Varanasi Art Festival, where artists showcased their best works, Kavya intended to ruin Aanya's reputation. She created a fake piece attributed to Aanya, filled with dark themes and twisted imagery, a stark contrast to Aanya's bright, uplifting style. The goal was to expose Aanya as a fraud, an artist who could only produce darkness when the spotlight shone on her.

As the festival opened, Aanya felt the familiar mix of excitement and nerves. She showcased her latest piece, a celebration of life along the Ganges. The crowd responded with applause, their admiration warming her heart. Yet, amidst the cheers, Kavya stood in the shadows, her heart racing with a toxic mix of thrill and dread.

Just as Kavya prepared to unveil her sinister plot, a sudden commotion erupted. Aanya's painting had been praised by a well-known critic, and she was invited to speak. Kavya's heart sank, knowing her plan would soon be exposed. At that moment, something within her snapped. Driven by rage, she rushed to the front of the crowd, ready to reveal her deceit.

"You're all fooled!" Kavya shouted, her voice cutting through the applause. "Aanya is nothing but a fraud! She can't even create her art!"

Gasps echoed through the crowd. Aanya turned, bewildered and hurt. "Kavya, what are you doing?"

"Tell them the truth! You're nothing without me!" Kavya's voice trembled, the weight of her envy spilling out in a chaotic storm. "I've been in your shadow long enough!"

Aanya's heart broke at her friend's desperation. "Kavya, I've never wanted to overshadow you. I've always believed in you. Why can't you see that?"

In that charged moment, something shifted. The crowd, initially taken aback, began to murmur. They recognized the pain and jealousy underlying Kavya's outburst, a reflection of her internal struggle.

Kavya felt a surge of panic as she realized the depths of her actions. Instead of gaining the attention she sought, she had exposed her vulnerability. With a trembling voice, she whispered, "I don't know how to be happy anymore."

Aanya stepped forward, her eyes filled with compassion. "Happiness isn't found in competition, Kavya. It's in celebrating our journeys. Let's help each other instead of tearing one another down."

The crowd, moved by Aanya's grace, began to applaud her words. At that moment, something shifted, not just for Kavya but for everyone present. The realization that envy destroys only the envier resonated deeply.

Kavya stood frozen, her heart pounding. As the weight of her actions sank in, tears streamed down her face. "I'm so sorry," she choked out. "I've let envy consume me. I don't want to be this way anymore."

The audience, touched by the raw honesty, began to cheer for both artists. In the days that followed, Kavya sought therapy and began to explore her style without the shadow of Aanya's success looming over her. Slowly, she rediscovered her passion for art, learning to embrace her unique voice.

Aanya, too, grew from the experience. She learned the importance of lifting others, and together, they collaborated on a series of paintings that celebrated their friendship, resilience, and the beauty of their shared journey.

In Varanasi, under the shimmering light of the Ganges, Aanya and Kavya painted a new chapter in their lives, transforming their once tumultuous relationship into a partnership that inspired many. They became symbols of growth, proving that while envy can eat away at one's heart, compassion and collaboration can heal even the deepest wounds.

In 'Paradise Lost', John Milton says, "Envy, like a serpent, eats its own heart."

It's often you, whether you would take Envy or Generosity. What will you choose: envy (resentment towards others' success) or generosity (willingness to celebrate others' achievements and gain peace)?

Son of Vinata

About the Author: Mouli Kr. Vasudeva
I am a lifelong enthusiast of ancient tales and timeless legends, captivated by the power of mythology. Through my writing, I aim to shine a light on the myths that have been lost to time, inviting my readers to explore these enchanting worlds filled with wonder and intrigue.

*****

Since I was little, I was very inquisitive and questioned everything around me and bombarded all those questions on my father, who always happily answered all of them. One such day, while I was sitting in the puja room randomly looking at all the framed photos of gods and goddesses, I looked at Lord Surya's picture of his charioteer, whose image was not so clear but visible enough for me to question it. I called out to my father, who was just passing by, pulled him into the puja room, and asked about the charioteer. He smiled at me, sat beside me, and began to narrate the hidden tale of the son of Vinata.

"Sage Kashyapa, as you know, is one of the seven holy rishis and father of all living species. Vinata and Kadru were two daughters of King Daksha who were married to Sage Kashyapa. One day he asked Vinata and Kadru to ask for a boon. Kadru asked for a thousand sons, and Vinata asked for two sons who would be stronger than all the sons of Kadru. In time both laid eggs, and soon Kadru's eggs hatched first, and the first nagas were born. Vinata, on the other hand, kept waiting, but her eggs showed no sign of hatching.

One day both the sisters went out for a stroll on the seashore, and Vinata spotted Uchaishravas, the seven-headed horse flying in the sky."

"Father, if I am right, this is the same horse who emerged from the churning of the ocean." I asked him.

"Yes, absolutely right." he affirmed.

"Vinata pointed out the horse to Kadru, exclaiming how white it was. But by the time Kadru looked up at the sky to spot the horse, he had galloped away in the darkness, and its tail was all Kadru was able to see. Since she had seen the horse's tail in the darkness, she claimed that it was black, but Vinata was pretty sure that the tail was white, so the two sisters decided to bet on it, and Kadru kept a condition that the one who won would keep the other one as their slave. Kadru knew she had made a mistake and that the horse's tail was white, but she was too proud to admit her mistake. That night she went to her children and asked for their help. She told them to cover Uchaishravas's tail, and since they are serpents, they would appear black from a distance. Most of her children opposed this and told her not to cheat on her sister, but Kadru was too determined to win the bet, and seeing her children deny her appeal, she cursed them with death, saying all of them would die in a Sarpa yagna. Only one naga agreed to help, and Kadru's plan came into action the next morning when Uchaishravas was spotted in the sky. Vinata, not suspecting anything, accepted her defeat and became her sister's slave. Kadru told Vinata that her slavery would end only when her son brought Amrita from Lord Indra for the nagas who would perish due to the yagna one day, and till then she would remain Kadru's slave. Poor Vinata had no other choice than to agree to the condition.

Years passed, and still, there was no sign of Vinata's eggs hatching. So overcome by frustration, she slightly broke open one of her eggs, and out of it emerged a beautiful boy who shone like a ray of the sun itself with magnificent wings and a strong upper body, but unfortunately his legs were undeveloped. The boy sorrowfully asked Vinata the reason for her hurry, to which Vinata remained silent with no answer. He further explained to Vinata that good things take time and patience, and since she had asked for her sons to be more powerful than a thousand serpents, it had to take time. Grief struck with the loss of his legs, and being unable to retrieve the nectar to free his mother, he cursed Vinata that her other egg would not hatch before another five hundred years and advised her to patiently wait this time. Vinata cried and asked for forgiveness, but it was too late. Her son bowed down to take her leave, but Vinata did not want to part with her son and told him that she wished to see him every day. And so, fulfilling his mother's only wish, he tells her that he will become the charioteer of Surya Deva and ride his seven horses from dawn to dusk. 'Every day I will accompany the sun god, and every morning I will be known as Aruna, and so you will be able to see me whenever you want to.', he said.

Vinata learned from the incident and waited for five hundred long years, and finally one day her egg hatched and out came a strong-winged, healthy boy with enormous strength and power. He was none other than The Mighty Garuda. He thanked Vinata for her patience, due to which he became so strong and healthy. He promised his mother to free her from slavery and soared high in the sky. Vinata looked up at him with pride, happiness, and a ray of hope in her eyes, which were to finally see her freedom."

"Wow!" I exclaimed. Mesmerized by the story I had heard. I was still curious, so I asked my father whether Garuda was able to free his mother. He smiled and gave a positive nod, patted my head, and left the room. He left that part of the story for another day and left for work.

Later, when I grew up, I realized the reason why the first rays of the morning are called Arunodaya—the coming of Aruna—and why Arunachal Pradesh is named so. Our culture is filled with such hidden tales that got forgotten over time, and it should be we who should bring these stories out and let everyone know about them because everything in India has a reason, and every reason has a hidden story behind it.

CHAPTER EIGHTEEN

The Lost Heir

About the Author: Muskan Singh
Hello! I'm Muskan Singh, an enthusiastic reader with a passion for fiction. I am thrilled to share my writing with you this time! In 7th grade, I was fortunate to be selected for the Quill Club Writers program, but I regrettably turned down the opportunity. Perhaps it was destiny that led me to another wonderful chance to showcase my story with the world. I am excited and happy to embark on this new journey!

*****

Lilian was a sweet and innocent child, the heart of the orphanage. Everyone adored her, showering her with love and affection. Tragically, two years ago, she lost her parents, Mr. and Mrs. Wilson, in a car accident when she was just five. Now, on her seventh birthday, the orphanage was alive with bright lights and decorations, filled with laughter and joy.

As the children sang and celebrated, a sudden gunshot shattered the bliss. Panic erupted, and people scrambled for safety as armed men in black stormed in, searching for one person: Lilian. Confusion gripped the crowd. What could a seven-year-old child possibly have to do with dangerous criminals?

Mrs. Greta, the caretaker, managed to call the police, but it was too late. Another shot rang out, and in the chaos, Lilian vanished.

The Search Begins

Three days later, the police uncovered a shocking truth. Lilian was not just any girl; she was the sole heir to the Smith family, the wealthiest in town. The realization struck like lightning—Lilian's real parents had been desperately searching for her all these years.

Eight years earlier, fate had played a cruel trick. Mrs. Wilson and Mrs. Smith were both admitted to the same hospital, where a mix-up occurred. Lilian had grown up in an orphanage while the Smiths raised a girl named Suzy, unaware of the switch. When the Smiths discovered the truth through a medical examination, they were devastated but chose to keep Suzy, showering her with love while they searched for their biological daughter.

Now, with the Smiths contacted by the kidnappers demanding half their fortune, the urgency escalated. The police quickly traced the kidnappers to an isolated island far from the mainland.

A Deeper Mystery

Detective George, a seasoned investigator with a reputation for uncovering hidden truths, sensed something more sinister at play. The kidnapping seemed less about money and more about revenge. The current leader of the Flying Eagles, a mafia organization, harboured a personal vendetta against the Smith family. Years ago, the Smiths had collaborated with the police to dismantle the previous mafia leadership, which had led to the arrest of the brother of the current leader.

Detective George's investigation revealed that the kidnapping was a ploy to lure the Smiths to the island, intending to eliminate them and erase their lineage. Time was running out.

The Stormy Rescue

The police organized a covert mission to the island, facing treacherous waves and relentless storms. As they neared the shore, the Smiths, fuelled by hope and determination, joined the rescue operation. Their love for Lilian drove them through the chaos.

After a harrowing journey, they arrived at the island. The confrontation with the kidnappers was intense. Detective George, with his sharp instincts, led the charge, using stealth to navigate the compound. Finally, they found Lilian, frightened but unharmed, locked in a room.

The Unexpected Twist

Just as they thought they had secured Lilian, the leader of the Flying Eagles emerged, revealing a shocking truth: the kidnapping was not just about money but a means to break the Smith family. The leader disclosed that he had been tracking the Smiths for years, waiting for the perfect moment to exact his revenge.

With a sinister smile, he revealed his plan to eliminate the Smiths and take control of their fortune, ensuring that no one would stand in his way. The stakes were higher than ever.

In a dramatic standoff, Detective George faced the leader, utilizing his wit and skill. As tensions escalated, the police surrounded the compound, forcing the kidnappers into a corner.

A Triumphant Return

In the end, Detective George's quick thinking led to the capture of the kidnappers, and Lilian was safely rescued. She was taken to the hospital, still shaken but relieved to be free.

When she opened her eyes, she saw Mrs. Smith gently stroking her hair. The reunion was filled with tears of joy as the Smiths embraced their long-lost daughter. The caretaker and children from the orphanage were overjoyed yet heartbroken to see their beloved Lilian leave.

But the Smiths promised to maintain ties with the orphanage, vowing to ensure that love and support continued for all the children there.

In the weeks that followed, Lilian adjusted to her new life, filled with warmth and love from her true family. Though she had faced unimaginable danger, she found comfort in the knowledge that she was home; at last, a lost heir was finally found.

CHAPTER NINETEEN

My Last Breath

About the Author: Rishika Ghoshal

I am Rishika Ghoshal, and I have a keen interest in exploring the world around me. My goal is to capture and share my learnings and experiences, inviting others to see the world through a different lens. Through my writing, I aspire to inspire readers to embrace new perspectives and appreciate the beauty in diversity.

*****

Life is like a long road, and we, as travelers, move from country to country, village to village, from being a child to becoming an elder. I've spent a long time in this world as a traveler, and now I take my last few breaths in this wonderful place. Lying on my deathbed, with a pen and notebook in hand, I want to write my whole life on these few pages. Every small detail, every joy, loss, and lesson deserves to be shared. For everyone, life is a lesson filled with heartbreaks, losses, and gains. Perhaps today's generation may find it hard to believe that such an old lady lived an extraordinary life. That's why I feel compelled to write.

My childhood was like anyone else's. As a little girl, my world revolved around my mother. Those were days of pure happiness, free from regrets, when everything seemed exciting. My mother was the most important person in my life. I often reflect on her and wrote this poem to express her essence:

"She was like the morning sunshine of January.
She was like the cherry blossoms of February.
She was like the warmth of March.
The blossoming flowers of May,
The longest day of June,
The clouds of August,
The peaceful silence of September,
On the deep nights of October,
The changes in November,
The coal-warmed evenings of December."

This poem captures my mother's nature. Thinking of those times still makes me laugh—crying over small things, like not wanting to go to school, and finding joy in every little moment. Time passed, and that small girl became a teenager. My teenage life was full of both suspense and trauma. I was often bullied, and it left me confused and hurt. At the time, I didn't understand why people around me always spoke poorly of me. Looking back now, I realize I was a good student and not bad-looking, yet still, I was hated.

I sat on the last bench, friendless, feeling as if no one loved or hated me—just ignored me. Those days were traumatizing for a 13-year-old girl. On top of it, my tuition teacher was abusive, hitting and scolding me for small mistakes. It felt like the world despised me, and inside, a hundred voices seemed to judge me. Those memories still have the power to bring me to tears, but now I can write about them with a sense of peace. God was always on my side, seeing my pain and offering relief. Changing schools turned my life around.

In the new school, everyone accepted me for who I was. It was the first time I felt supported and unjudged. I made many friends and began to enjoy my school days, growing more confident and shedding my insecurities. I embraced the idea of being imperfectly perfect. My teenage years were filled with emotions, including the excitement of my first crush at 15. Even though I wasn't lucky enough to have that special someone in my life, I wrote a poem to express my feelings:

"Out of my hundred thoughts, you are ninety-nine,
I share a million dreams with you in my imagination.
But never say a word to you in reality.
Though I know our love may be one-sided,
I will cherish these feelings until my last breath.
But it hurts that you have time for everyone but me.
I ask God why I cannot have you.
And God replies, 'Because he never asked for you.'"

Reading that now makes me smile, but I know everyone's first love leaves a lasting imprint on the heart. My school days flew by, and soon it was time for college. I went to one of the best colleges in Delhi and began preparing for my CA exams. But fate had other plans—on the day of my exam, I got stuck in heavy traffic and missed the test. At the time, it felt like the end of the world, and I even had thoughts of suicide. But through writing, I found a way to express my pain and heal. I wrote:

"I don't remember the present; I live in the past,
Walking on a path without knowing where I'm going.
I travel from country to country, from village to village.
Not just walking the roads, but experiencing them.
Perhaps the roads know the dreams I chase."

Though I missed the CA exam, I eventually accepted that God had a different path for me. I completed my

Economics Honours and found a wonderful job. In my mid-20s, I suffered another deep loss when one of my closest friends passed away from cancer. Her absence left me feeling empty, like part of me had vanished. I penned these words for her:

"That vanished hand touched my heart.

Leaving a thousand memories behind.

From our first meeting to our last goodbye,

The tears in my eyes can never bring you back.

The best gift of my life disappeared into the purple sky,

Tearing me apart like a gray, stormy day."

Losing her was painful, but it taught me the art of detachment. I accepted the reality of her passing and moved on, continuing my journey of growth. It was during this time that the most unexpected thing happened—love entered my life in the form of an arranged marriage. At first, I resisted, but when I met him, I knew he was the one. His gentle smile, warm eyes, and kind spirit drew me in. It was as if the man I had dreamed of stood before me, and we spent 50 beautiful years together. He was my rock, my partner, my best friend. We laughed, cried, and built a lifetime of memories.

Now, as a 78-year-old woman, I look back with a heart full of gratitude. Life, with all its imperfections and surprises, has been a beautiful journey. My advice? Never chase perfection. Embrace your perfectly imperfect self, take every opportunity to learn, and follow your heart's desires. And now, as I close my eyes, I do so with peace, knowing I've lived fully. Now I want to close my eyes forever.

CHAPTER TWENTY

Shadow of Justice

About the Author: Sabhyata Singh
Born on January 9, 2007, in Varanasi, I am Sabhyata Singh, the youngest in a family that includes my father, a dedicated government employee, my mother, a talented homemaker, and my elder brother, an engineer. I have a passion for journaling, expressing my thoughts through both writing and drawing. An aficionado of retro music, I enjoy discovering underrated artists that inspire my creativity. Known as the "creative wizard" among my peers, I indulge in painting, sketching, and craft work. My ultimate aspiration is to soar through the skies as a pilot.

*****

No crime cases had been reported in the past few days. It seemed as though even lawbreakers had decided to take a break. My duty for the day was officially over, though I hadn't really done anything the entire time apart from dozing off in my chamber. Now, I was getting ready to head home.

It was a pitch-black winter night, and the crisp, biting air struck my face as it flowed through the car's slightly rolled-down window. The roads were desolate, with not a soul in sight. Darkness and silence had never unnerved me; in fact, I welcomed them. As I drove along the empty stretch, struggling to keep my eyes open, my fellow officer, sitting in the passenger seat, was snoring away, completely oblivious to everything around him.

His days at work were always hectic, but not for the reasons you might expect. He had grown weary of charging people for minor offenses, instead taking bribes to look the other way. In his twisted philosophy, "If it paid well, it was legal." I despised his lack of ethics, but I'd learned that corruption thrives without needing anyone's approval.

As I continued driving, my headlights illuminated something in the distance—a large, dark figure standing ominously in the middle of the road. At first, I dismissed it as a tree or some sort of shadow. But as I got closer, the figure became clearer, though still too indistinct to identify. I slowed the car to a stop, debating whether to step out and investigate or take a detour. The latter option would cost me more time, and all I wanted was to get home and sleep.

Reluctantly, I got out of the car. The cold air wrapped around me, and with each step I took toward the shadowy figure, an unsettling feeling began to creep in. Despite my usual courage, I couldn't shake the growing fear in my chest. The figure became more defined yet no less perplexing—it resembled a human, but its body appeared to be made of swirling black clouds. Its head was formless, with only vague facial features, while its limbs seemed solid enough to discern.

Suddenly, I noticed the figure bending down, as though picking something up. It was gathering pieces of gold scattered on the ground. I froze, trying to process what I was seeing. Just as quickly as it had appeared, the figure vanished into thin air, leaving me standing there, paralyzed by a spine-chilling fear.

I rushed back to the car, my hands trembling as I gripped the steering wheel. My entire body was shivering, though not from the cold. My fellow officer remained sound asleep, completely unaware of the bizarre encounter I had just experienced. I dropped him off at his house and finally drove to mine, but sleep eluded me that night. Every time I closed my eyes, the image of the shadowy figure and the glinting gold pieces haunted me.

The next morning, I woke up groggy and unsettled, still mulling over the events of the previous night. I left for the police station, unaware that the day ahead held more chilling surprises. On my way, my phone buzzed with a call that made my blood run cold.

"The officer passed away this morning," the voice on the other end said.

I was so shaken by the news that I didn't even think to ask what had caused his death. My thoughts were a chaotic mess as I reached the station, but the scene that greeted me there only added to the confusion. Smoke hung in the air like a thick, suffocating veil. The floors were coated in ash, and the walls had been blackened by soot. It was clear that a fire had broken out during the night, but strangely, only the prisoners' cells had been affected.

As I joined the investigation, I stumbled upon something that made my stomach churn—a few scattered gold pieces, eerily similar to the ones I had seen the previous night. Beside them lay a note, written in jagged, almost otherworldly handwriting:

"People are involved in illicit activities, making this world a miserable place to live. As long as it continues to be a miserable place, I'll feed on those who make it so."

Before I could fully absorb the meaning of the note, a constable approached me, his face pale. "Sir, we found similar gold pieces near the body of the officer who died this morning," he reported.

In that instant, everything clicked—the shadowy figure, the gold, the officer's death, and the fire that had only targeted the prisoners. It all pointed to something far beyond human understanding. The station buzzed with murmurs as officers exchanged theories, their voices tinged with fear and confusion.

One constable turned to me and asked, "You were with him last night. What do you think happened?"

I opened my mouth to respond but found myself at a loss for words. How could I explain something so unreal? The truth felt too bizarre to share, yet it was undeniable—some supernatural force was at work, exacting justice for the wrongs that had gone unpunished.

As I stood there amidst the chaos, a strange sense of calm washed over me. The loud chatter around me faded into silence, leaving me with one thought: justice was being served, but not by human hands.

CHAPTER TWENTY-ONE

The Diary Entry

About the Author: Sakhi

Sakhi is an 11th-grade student born on July 22, 2008, in Varanasi. She has a keen interest in sketching and reading, with a particular fondness for the works of John Green, her favorite author. Through her artistic and literary pursuits, Sakhi explores the world around her, blending creativity with a love for storytelling.

*****

4th August, 2023

Dear Diary,

Today was also just like how other Fridays are boring and tiring. I got scolded by my boss again. The reason you may ask was because I hadn't handed over the work he gave me. All I mean to say is, How can he even expect me to complete a task in such insufficient time?

I live alone in the house of my parents, the only remaining property I have, of my family. Sometimes I feel like I was the one responsible for their death, "the bad luck bearer," as I was called by my high school classmates. But the only one I had all my life since 6th grade was Rose, my best friend. The one who took care of me and stood up for me when I was unable to. And that reminds me why I started writing this entry.

Rose had paid me a surprise visit this morning. She would

be staying here with me for a while as she recently quit her corporate job. I was so happy to see her after so long. Seeing her, I'm immediately reminded of our college days, when we used to live together and have fun.

We went out to have dinner as she was kind of new to this place. About an hour ago, we came back to my parent's house, and we decided to watch a movie together and enjoy every moment we could, till we were together.

I think I'm getting even more eager to watch the movie with her, so hereby I rest my pen. I'll come and update you tomorrow.

Good night!!

   ***

"Did you decide which movie we are going to watch?" asks Emma while opening the door to an empty room. "Huh? Where did she go?" walking towards the other rooms and the bathroom. "Rose! Rose! Where are you, Rose?" She shouts, looking for her, when suddenly a distant door slams shut. She immediately turns towards the door and walks forward. Holding the doorknob hesitantly, she asks one last time, "Rose, is it you?". She flies open the door to see nothing but darkness. She takes a few steps inside the room to turn on the lights, but she is turned on forcefully in the dark room when suddenly dim lights turn on, revealing a person with black attire and a face well hidden by masks and glasses. The person had a sharp knife in one hand. Emma immediately turns pale and tries to ask the person in a monotonous tone, "W-who are you??"

Revealing their face, the person speaks up. "Admit it, you are scared for your life. Don't try to act tough."

Emma, in utter shock, manages to ask, "Rose??? What is this?? This is a horrible prank idea, okay?"

"Tsk- tsk- you sure are very dumb" Rose speaks up as she moves the knife towards Emma's neck, holding it a few inches away.

"Is this not a joke, Rose?" her eyes fixed on the knife.

"It never was, dear" Rose says as she laughs wickedly.

"This is scary!! Please, Rose, stop this. Why are you doing this?" She bursts out crying.

"Ha Ha, I had to" laugh evilly. "Because of your stingy family, my family was ruined."

Flashback

Emma's family owned a big chemical company and were very rich. Rose's parents, being poor, worked in the company with minimal safety measures. One night, due to a toxic chemical leak in the manufacturing block of the company, hundreds of workers died the same night, among which were Rose's parents. This all could have been avoided if James, Emma's late father, had provided funds for necessary safety measures.

"If only your stingy father had allowed sufficient safety measures, my parents would still be alive with me!! I was 9 years old when I lost them!! All because of your family! That's why I decided the night I lost my parents to take their revenge. Only you are left," admits Rose.

"W-what do you mean? My family died in a car accident," questions Emma flabbergasted.

"You are still so dull-witted. It was me, your dear best friend Rose, the cause of the ruin of your family line," Rose says in sarcasm.

Emma looks in horror. "You ??"

"Mm-hmm",

Both hear a loud noise and are taken off guard for a while. As Rose lowers the knife subconsciously, Emma manages to run towards the door, closing it from outside but starts crying hysterically, unable to make out what to do next. She turns back alarmed as she hears footsteps approaching her when she sees Eden, her work friend.

"Are you okay?" he asks.

"N-no, I'm not," she starts crying again. "How did you come here?"

"I called you several times; we have to turn in the project tomorrow. You didn't pick up my call, and so I was naturally worried. I heard you crying from the living room and decided to come here," he says.

"I thank you so much. I'll try my best to repay my gratitude, but for now, please help me," she pleads.

"Well, okay, what do you need help with?"

"Just know this for now; there is a person inside this room who wants to kill me," she says, shaking with fear.

"I should call the police; let them handle this while you stay away from here."

"Hmm," she nods her head.

A few months later, Rose got arrested by the police for attempting to murder. Emma is back to her life; she had a psychological impact because of that incident, but it's of no account in her daily life. She now lives in a rented house with her pet cat, gifted by Eden. The old house is left for sale.

A day before, Emma was called by a family that was interested in buying the house. Emma is on her way to the house with Eden to grab a few things she has left behind in that house since that incident.

The car pulls over in front of the entry door when Emma and Eden get out.

"Let's put an end to this," Emma says as she half smiles.

"Yup," Eden nods.

She moves to her room to grab her diary, which she wrote

daily till the 4th of August, and a few of her family members' photographs, which were hung on the wall beside her bed. She clutches the photographs as she takes them down from the wall when Eden asks to hold them for her. She moves to her table, where her diary covered with dust is kept. She picks up her diary and immediately blows the dust away to look at her diary entries briefly. She skims the pages until she lands on the diary entry of 4th August, a day that traumatized her. She notices a folded, crinkly page peeking from the next page. . As she slides it out she is horrified to such an extent that the diary she once loved dearly slipped and felln onto the dusty floor because the page had in the handwriting she very well remembered written–
21st January, 2024
Missed me?

CHAPTER TWENTY-TWO

Mirrors of Revenge

About the Author: Samyak Tiwari
Residing in the vibrant city of Varanasi, I am Samyak Tiwari. My mother is a dedicated homemaker, while my father is a professor at BHU. My passion for reading and writing was sparked by my best friend, Shaurya. I consider myself a polyglot programmer, skillfully navigating multiple programming languages. Alongside storytelling, I also explore poetry, which has deepened my appreciation for literature. As I continue this journey, I eagerly await the opportunities and adventures life has in store for me.

*****

He kneeled and presented her with flowers. She had tears in her eyes. The dream both once saw together was finally happening.

"The kingdom never sleeps," they say about Samraathgarh. A kingdom full of hubbub, the crowd had a new reason to celebrate. Their one and only beloved king was getting married to the love of his life.

Khushwant Kajar, king of the most powerful kingdom of his era, "Samraathgarh," was one just king. The bravest and strongest ruler of his empire had never lost even a single battle since he was crowned at the young age of 16. But this honourable king had a weakness, and that was his beloved Hiya.

Hiya was the queen of Ghatsaraj (Kingdom of Ghats). Penning down her beauty would be no less than a crime itself. Hair like a dark forest, voice like a calm ocean. She was like a snowflake in a storm. Her eyes held the depth of a thousand mirrors, capturing both the warmth of the palace and the cool serenity of a starlit night. Her movements were graceful, like the flicker of candlelight dancing across the mirrored surfaces, soft yet captivating.

Khushwant Kajar's love for Hiya was no secret. Hiya was far more than just a weakness to Khushwant. It was said that even in the heat of battle, the thought of her radiant smile gave him strength, and her name, a whispered prayer on his lips, gave him vigour for a brawl. Hiya was not just a queen but his anchor.

Although Ghatsaraj was a smaller kingdom compared to Samraathgarh, its importance lay in more than its size. Its ghats were sacred, drawing pilgrims from distant lands, and its people revered Hiya as much for her wisdom as for her beauty.

She ruled with grace, a balance to Khushwant's fierce might. Together, they were unstoppable—his sword, her spirit.

Their marriage was one big jamboree in the kingdom. Streets were lit and decorated.

The king and queen were blessed by the older ones in the kingdom.

With the great "Ganesh Puja," the date of marriage was finalized.

Both looked at each other and shared a sight of comfort. But who knew this was just silence before the storm? What beheld the future of the kingdom and the life of the couple was unpredictable.

Khushwant, as a sign of love and gratitude towards Hiya, gifted her a "Sheeshmahal" (the Palace of Mirrors).

Walls glittering and shining with a million reflections. The glass catches the rays of the sun and casts vibrant hues of multiple colors across its boundaries. Handcrafted and delicately carved pillars by expert masons. Ceilings engraved with delicate mosaic mirrors. Beautifully made chandeliers hang like delicate raindrops amidst a snowfall. Crystals are placed in a manner that reflects the image of snowflakes. The hall is over lighted and shimmering. The Sheeshmahal reflected not just its beauty but also the graze and empowerment of the king and his love for Hiya.

Meanwhile, in Samraathgarh, the arrangements were made and royal families and facilities were made ready. World-famous musicians, classical dancers, and artists from all over the world were invited. The whole city was looking no less than a bride itself. But Hiya had different plans for herself for the night. The night before their marriage, instead of staying in the palace for the night, she made arrangements for herself in the Sheeshmahal to stay the night among the stars and moon and look at the millionth reflection of millions of stars in the mirrors.

But who knew this one decision of hers would cost her an arm and leg, or rather, I say, would cost her life?

The next morning, the maids of the mahal found Hiya's body in the mirror labyrinth of the Sheesh mahal with a dagger in her left chest.

Khushwant Kajar was immediately informed of the same, and for him, his whole world collapsed. He headed straight to the Sheeshmahal, entering in the Mahal; his eyes flooded out; the one who gave him his strength was lying in front of him, lifeless.

The amount of grief he felt at the moment was unspeakable.

I still remember when I first entered Samraathgarh. I felt that this place held a lot of secrets, quite ironic for a place like this that never sleeps.

When I arrived at the palace, I was immediately escorted to the Sheeshmahal. Ever seen heaven? I did that day. The beauty of the Mahal ever mentioned was way lesser and could never be more than how beautiful it was. A single vibrant ray of sun was used to disperse into millions of fragments, enhancing the crystals embedded.

The time I first saw Khushwant Kajar, he was held for words. Wiping in grief, no one else other than him could ever understand. Anyway, I asked people to clear the site. The minister escorted him out while holding and consoling him.

This is when I noticed that Minister's Scabbard on the left was a little loose, hence helping him to fix it. While fixing it, I saw the minister miss his left thumb. I wanted to ask him the reason but eventually settled on asking it later.

After King's departure, I got to my work and was interrogated. The weird part was no stranger or known entered the premises or left it since last night. "This place definitely holds a story worth telling," I thought to myself.

After a long day of work, I finally decided to meet the king and the minister. Hence, I went straight into the King's room. He was deep asleep, and after getting to know that his health was not quite pink, I thought this wasn't the correct time to ask him questions. Therefore, I finally decided to meet the minister.

When I entered the minister's room, I found him weeping.

"Are you crying?" I asked, "What's the matter?"?

"Me"? He replied, "Weeping? No, and even if I were, the tears are all dry now.".

Anyway, after a long session of cross-questioning, I finally asked him, "Why do you miss a thumb on the left?"?

"Oh, it was during a battle in the south that I lost my thumb during a sword fight." He replied.

After all this, I finally decided to call off the day for me. For now,

I had 4 major suspects. Jayesh, the guard of Hiya's room,

Kathiyawali, Hiya's maid; Umesh, caretaker of the palace; and Raju, the boatman who brought people from land to Sheeshmahal.

I was all indulged in this case. But being honest, it was the toughest one ever. Day by day, new clues were being discovered, and useful ones created a whole new perspective on the case. After a week of investigation, I was brought to where I started. Nothing.

It was my last day in Samraathgarh. I felt a little bad; the 100th case failed. But I felt even worse for the king. So, for the last time, I went inside his room to take a look at him.

"Oh Samay," he greeted me. "Did you find any leads?"?

"I am sorry, my lord, I couldn't." I apologized, "I failed my case this time.".

"Oh, don't feel sorry," he said. "It is me who failed. I failed as a man to protect my love. Failed as an emperor, to be able to give my empire their queen, even after being the king of the strongest kingdom of my era, couldn't even save my love. I am the failure; you were just doing your job, and you gave it all in.".

I consoled him and left his room. Now I was feeling guilty for giving up so early. I still had the whole night ahead. "Like I am Samay, I can do this. 99 cases, none of them missed. I am the best". What was I missing? With all these thoughts, I went back to the place where it all began, "THE SHEESHMAHAL.".

The moment I entered it, I was welcomed with a light, eerie blow of wind on my face, as if the Queen herself were trying to ask for her justice.

I went back to the place where she was murdered. A broken mirror, flickering lights, and gloominess were all that was left in this place, which once represented joy. I was walking back and forth, thinking and giving it all in.

"Come on, what am I missing?" I asked myself "It's Sheeshmahal, Light never fades here, how can no one ever see the killer arrive or departure".

I was busy thinking all this when I suddenly noticed the mirror in front of which the queen was murdered. The mirror was different. Could it be an answer to all my questions? I bent down to grab it. "Bingo!" I yelled, "This mirror indeed is different from the others." After this, I started comparing it with the other mirrors in Sheeshmahal. Guess what? The one I was holding was thicker than the usual mirror.

"A two-way mirror," it struck me. "Yes!! No one ever saw him enter because he never did. He was always there, in front of them, just that they couldn't ever see him.".

What else can I conclude from this? Come on, I had to do it now. Also, the murderer was important to the kingdom. Otherwise, there was no way he knew about the mirror, and even if he knew, he couldn't ever blend in with them.

After observing a lot at the location, I think I got it. The dagger was the answer to all my questions. The weapon of murder, the dagger, was held in an icepick position and reversed towards the blunter side. This was not normal.

Because a left-handed killer would've stabbed the victim with a sharper edge towards himself and a right-handed killer would've attacked on the right chest. Also, the fingers curled were reversed, which means the murder was done by someone who was right-handed. But the question of not attacking the right chest kept me busy for a moment before I realized "It is Sheeshmahal, the mirror on the back reversed the perspective of the killer and he stabbed the queen on the left instead of right". After an intense observation and analysis of finger patterns, I guess I cracked the case.

I immediately headed towards the palace and entered the king's room. "Sir, I guess I cracked the case," I said. "The murderer was right-handed and wanted it to be framed as left-handed. There were only four marks that were reversed, meaning the knife was held in the left hand in the icepick position. The only mark of one finger was missing, the left grip thumb."

"What do you want to say?" He asked, "Is it..." I nodded in agreement position.

He was immediately called up to the court.

"Why, Minister, why would you do it to me?" King asked, almost breaking down, "I considered you as my father figure.".

"Hiya," he replied with a deep and heavy breath. "Hiya was the reason; she got what she paid for.".

Before the matter got serious, he was asked to open up about what he was saying.

"Well," he started, "Khushwant, do you remember Shivani?"?

"Yes," Khushwant replied, "your traitor daughter who was executed.".

"It was a murder," the minister yelled.

"What do you mean"? Khushwant asked, unable to hold up the suspense.

Shivani Gupta, daughter of the Minister. An extraordinary girl, with the voice of a nightingale and well known for her singing in the kingdom at the time when Khushwant's father, Mahid, used to rule over Samraathgarh. Acing the art of battle with full knowledge of sword fighting, archery, and spear battle. She was not just an ordinary girl; she was an apple of Mahid's eye. He treated her just like his own daughter.

Khushwant and Shivani were best friends during their childhood. They used to sword fight and play together all the time. Shining stars of the royal palace. But one person was disgusted by this friendship: Hiya.

Hiya's father, Harpreet, was an ally of Samraathgarh since Mahid saved Ghatsaraj from an invasion. This is when Hiya came to Samraathgarh for the first time. She was all alone and gloomy when she met Shivani. Soon they started to spend a lot of time together and became blossom buds in no less time.

It was a pleasant morning in the royal palace of Samraathgarh.

Khushwant was practicing shooting apples on the nearby tree with his bow. Suddenly he heard a loud yell, "KHUSHWANT." He recognized it. "SHIVANI," he yelled back.

Shivani ran towards Khushwant along with Hiya. It was Hiya's first time seeing Khushwant, and her eyes lingered on him.

Khushwant smiled brightly at Shivani, and the two exchanged playful banter as they always did. Their laughter echoed through the gardens, drawing sharp contrast with Hiya's increasingly watchful gaze. From the moment she set her eyes on Khushwant, Hiya felt something stir inside her. Something she had never experienced before. It wasn't just Khushwant's charm that captivated her, but the ease with which Shivani seemed to share every part of his life. She felt jealous.

As the days passed, Hiya's jealousy only deepened. She watched from the shadows as Shivani and Khushwant spent time together, sharing inside jokes, secret glances, and stories that only lifelong friends could. Hiya began to imagine herself in Shivani's place, dreaming of what it would be like to have Khushwant's attention and affection all to herself.

Driven by envy, Hiya decided she could not stand by any longer. She began to weave a subtle plot, her mind calculating and her heart full of bitterness. Hiya whispered rumours into the ears of the courtiers, sowing seeds of doubt about Shivani's intentions toward Khushwant. She portrayed Shivani as a manipulative woman who sought to control Khushwant and undermine the kingdom. Slowly but surely, these whispers began to take root, especially among those who were already wary of Shivani's close relationship with Khushwant.

Hiya played her role perfectly, presenting herself as an innocent one, only concerned for the well-being of the palace and its young prince. The gossip spread quickly, and soon the palace was filled with talk of Shivani's supposed ambitions. Tensions mounted, and Shivani, once beloved by many, found herself under increasing scrutiny.

It wasn't long before the rumours reached the ears of the royal council. They summoned Shivani for questioning, demanding explanations for her close relationship with Khushwant. Though she tried to defend herself, her words fell on deaf ears. The council, influenced by the growing tide of mistrust, began to consider drastic action. A recommendation was made to the king: Shivani should be banished from Samraathgarh; her presence was deemed a threat to the prince and the stability of the kingdom.

Shivani was devastated, not understanding how things had spiralled so quickly. Khushwant, too, was taken aback, shocked by the accusations against his friend. He was sheer shocked by the allegations. Shivani's fate was sealed, and since that day, Khushwant considered Shivani to be a traitor.

The incident was narrated to Khushwant by the minister about how Hiya, with her evil wit, got poor and innocent Shivani executed.

Khushwant was expressionless; he got betrayed by his love, and whom he considered to be a traitor for his whole life was actually innocent.

"HANG HIM," the king ordered, and started weeping to tears after losing another family-like father figure. My work was done here. 100th case, solved. But was it worth it?

I guess yes. When leaving the sight, what I saw was worth a hundred sights.

I saw the king near Hiya's grave.

He kneeled and presented her with flowers. He had tears in his eyes.

CHAPTER TWENTY-THREE

The Mirrors Whisper

About the Author: Sanskriti Singh
I am a curious soul, constantly seeking knowledge and personal growth. With a passion for life's intricacies, I strive to improve every day, embracing challenges along the way while remaining grounded in my core values.

*****

Lila always found solace in old things. So, when she moved into her grandmother's abandoned house after her passing, she wasn't frightened by the creaking floors or the shadows that danced in the dim light. She was comforted by the familiar scent of lavender and the delicate lace curtains that fluttered gently in the breeze. In the attic, she discovered a large, ornate mirror, covered in a thick layer of dust. The woodwork was intricate, with vines and flowers carved into the frame, and it seemed oddly out of place in the dusty, cobweb-filled attic. Lila, enamoured by its beauty, decided to clean it and hang it in her bedroom. That night, as she lay in bed, she heard a faint whisper. It was so soft that she almost dismissed it as the wind. But the whisper grew louder, more insistent. She turned on the light and looked around, but there was nothing—just the mirror reflecting her puzzled face. In the days that followed, the whispering continued. It wasn't just at night anymore. The whispers began to follow her throughout the house, growing louder whenever she was near the mirror. It was as if the mirror was calling out to her, demanding her attention. One evening, unable to bear it any longer, Lila stood in front of the mirror and stared into her reflection. The whispers turned into words, clear and desperate. "Help me..."Lila's heart raced. The voice wasn't hers. It was a woman's voice, filled with sorrow and pain. She tried to look away, but something held her gaze. As she looked deeper into the mirror, her reflection began to change. The familiar face she saw every day faded, replaced by the image of a woman she had never seen before. Her eyes were hollow, and her face was twisted in agony. Lila stumbled back, her hand flying to her mouth to stifle a scream. But she couldn't look away. The woman's lips moved, forming the words that echoed in Lila's mind: "Find me." Desperate to escape, Lila covered the mirror with a blanket and fled the room. But even then, she couldn't shake the feeling that the woman's eyes were still on her, watching, waiting. That night, Lila had a dream—or was it a nightmare? She was in the house, but it was different. The walls were cracked, the air thick with the stench of decay. She wandered through the halls, following the sound of weeping. It led her to the attic, where the mirror stood, uncovered. In the reflection, she saw the woman again. This time, she wasn't alone. A shadowy figure loomed behind her, its hands resting on her shoulders, its face hidden in darkness. The woman turned her tear-streaked face towards Lila, her eyes pleading. "He trapped me," she whispered. "He's coming for you." Lila woke with a start, her heart pounding in her chest. She could still hear the woman's voice and feel the cold dread that had settled in her bones. Determined to end the nightmare, she decided to research the mirror's origins. She discovered that the mirror had been in the family for generations, passed down from mother to daughter. But its history was shrouded in mystery. No one knew where it had come from or how it had ended up in the attic. Lila dug deeper, uncovering old letters and diaries, piecing together a story that chilled her to the core. Years ago, her great-great grandmother, a young woman named Evelyn, had been engaged to a man who was deeply possessive and jealous. When she tried to leave him, he cursed her, trapping her spirit in the mirror and dooming her to an eternity of suffering. The letters spoke of how Evelyn's presence in the mirror tormented her family for years until they finally hid it away, hoping to forget the horror. But the curse could never be forgotten. The mirror's hold was too strong, and it waited patiently for someone to release it. Lila knew what she had to do. With trembling hands, she uncovered the mirror and stared into it one last time. The woman's face appeared, more desperate than ever. "Free me," she begged. Lila took a deep breath and smashed the mirror with all her strength. The glass shattered into a million pieces, and for a moment, silence filled the room. Then, a soft sigh, almost of relief, drifted through the air, and the pieces of glass dissolved into dust. The house seemed lighter after that; the air was clearer. The whispers were gone, and for the first time in days, Lila felt at peace. But as she prepared to leave the house for good, she noticed something strange. In the corner of the room, where the mirror had once hung, there was a small, untouched shard of glass. And in it, a pair of hollow eyes watched her leave.

CHAPTER TWENTY-FOUR

The Shadows of Hollow Creek

About the Author: Saumy Vats

I'm Saumy Vats, an 18-year-old class XII student with a curious mind. I love exploring new hobbies, reading, and writing stories to express my thoughts and emotions. Describing myself as a 'jack of all trades I find joy in learning a little bit of everything while embracing the endless journey of storytelling.

*****

I left the car and descended onto the streets in the village of Hollow Creek, where my child's laughter echoed once. But right now, an uneasy quietness hung in the air, only the rustling of leaves punctuating the silence. The revitalized town shrinks into a haunting environment as if it's a picture held by frozen time. As a keen detective, I have come back to Hollow Creek to figure out the conversion behind the number of missing people. Each event was full of strange happenings that had left the citizens of the town bewildered and terrified. The old diner, once a nice place, was like a tomb in which the patrons' worried and secretive faces seemed to be engraved."

Marjorie, the elderly owner, greeted me with a solemn nod.

"Good to see you, Fredrick. But it's not a bright spot in our lives. Folks are just cycling out, and no one knows where or why. It's like the town has been cursed."

I looked up at the old woman with a questioning look in my eyes upon hearing her mention a curse. My search for clues was taking me to the old Willson's castle, the abode where my family lived, that has now been deserted. Amid my search, I stumbled upon some of my family's old things and a riddle-encoded ledger that pointed to a forgotten family secret.

Due to my trying to find the information, I came across the diary of my great-uncle Elias, containing bits of conversation about the "dark pact" formed with the spirits. I spoke with the records keeper Arthur Blake, who unveiled the fact that the Willson family previously made a deal with an enigmatic promoter to gain their fortune. Meanwhile, they were promissory to an archaic curse that required intermittent killings.

While doing thorough research, I came across a malevolent plot. A super-clandestine strategist of the village community had scheduled the vanishment, the mere appearance of which was used to hoodwink their brother townsfolk and ensure the town's good fortune was under control. As it turned out, my family too was to blame, although they were forced to make that pledge unbeknownst to them.

When the ultimate verity was out in the open, I audaciously challenged the town elders; consequently, the counterfeit curse was exposed, and the elders were detained. The stillness that had fallen over Hollow Creek was insignificantly interrupted by the newborn sense of optimism and fellowship.

Over a period of time, I went about revealing the riddle of the vanishments as well as setting my family and the town free from the evil, fearful truth. To repair the damage, Hollow Creek recovered from its dark period and gained a new, bright future.

The Shadows of Hollow Creek: The Lost Heirloom

Two town elders who had been arrested months ago were rebuilding Hollow Creek. I had unraveled the verbiage where I had added to it by sewing a veil of secrecy that covered my tracks. The first to approach me, with an anxious look in her expression, was Marjorie, the aged woman in charge of the local canteen. "Fredrick, I need your help. My grandmother's antique locket, which was passed down in the family through generations, has gone missing. It's not just any locket; it's said to hold a piece of Hollow Creek's history".

Drawn to the intrigue, I accepted the case. I began with the staff and guests of the restaurant I had initially inquired about, but no one provided any clues about the lost locket. Undeterred, I decided to pursue the search further, suspecting it might be tied to the town's history. My investigation eventually led me to the Willson Mansion, a house shrouded in mystery, with a secret room hidden deep within its basement. Inside, I discovered several cryptic letters and an old journal written by my great-uncle Elias. The journal hinted at a long-buried family feud, a secret that had been concealed for decades.

As I delved deeper into the investigation, unexpected revelations came to light. The locket was no longer a simple family heirloom; it had become the key to uncovering a secret that had been hidden for centuries. This secret, pieced together with the insights of Arthur Blake, the town historian, had the potential to alter the course of Hollow Creek's history forever. The locket revealed my great-uncle Elias's vision of a looming threat—a powerful organization that had been exploiting Hollow Creek for centuries, operating from the shadows.

However, I was not the only one on the hunt for the locket. A rival treasure hunter, known under the alias "The Shadow," joined the hunt. The opponent used implements of destruction and charged machinery along with the hustle for the locket. Indeed, we were in a game-afoot, and I was struck in a wild chase of truth-finding and protection of the future of Hollow Creek.

After much effort and meticulous examination, the matted papers, sealed letters, and diaries of Elias, combined with Arthur's research, added a new layer of understanding to the story of the locket. It had been hidden within an archaeological layer dating back to the city's founding era, in a location described by an ancient architectural relic that had long been forgotten. This discovery led us to an abandoned, overgrown graveyard situated in the farthest corner of the town. Beneath the fractured concrete of a crumbling tomb, we unearthed a concealed corridor that descended into a hidden grotto. The area was in disarray, strewn with artifacts from ancient times.

Amid the chaos, a pedestal stood prominently, supporting an ornate chest. As we approached the chest, a faint click echoed behind us. Turning around, we were confronted by a figure emerging from the shadows, clad in a dark mask and a vivid orange Stola adorned with a black sash. Their ominous presence made it clear they had no intention of letting us leave with the locket without a fight. A fierce and bitter struggle ensued as we fought to uncover and protect the remaining pieces of the enigma while fending off our relentless pursuers.

In terms of strength and skill, the shadowy figure proved to be a formidable match. However, with Arthur's cunning and my unwavering resolve, we ultimately managed to overpower them, secure the chest, and put an end to their pursuit. The locket, it seemed, held significant importance to the remaining documents we uncovered, which revealed the full extent of a vast conspiracy. These discoveries proved invaluable in piecing together the truth.

It became evident that powerful vested interests were at play—those of the former controlling elite of the town. During the earliest periods of its history, these elites operated almost entirely in the shadows. Through a combination of backdoor maneuvers and a web of deceit, they sought to extract valuable resources and wealth from the town for their own gain. The locket, it was said, contained the final piece of the puzzle—a key that, once uncovered, would render their plans futile and expose the true purpose behind their schemes with startling clarity.

We had the locket in our possession and headed once more to Hollow Creek, now armed with the truth that needed to be made known to the townspeople. It has always been shocking, but despite all that, the case has been resolved, and people started to heal a little and feel the appropriate bit of justice being served. The Shadow was captured, and their attempts to take over the town were thwarted.

When Hollow Creek was in the process of reconstruction, the necklace was kept safe in the hands of Marjorie, who placed it at the local museum, however so that the history of the ornament would not diminish in value. This time, townsmen had a much better tomorrow, free of the shadows that waited to swallow their development.

It would, at last, come to be abundantly evident that where the locket was as a mere family piece of jewelry, there was also the inner strength that defied all that sought to destabilize Hollow Creek and to uncover and reveal to this world the veiled truth.

CHAPTER TWENTY-FIVE

Rage of the Immortals

About the Author: Shaurya Srivastava

Shaurya Srivastava is a creative being from Varanasi. He grasps inspiration from abstract sources and evolves creative solutions to life. This creativity is often found blossoming in the pages of Shaurya's books and stories. Full of twists and turns, the reader is compelled to derive their own understanding of the story's motives and message to the real world.

*****

Somewhere in the Arthur Hills... Suddenly, the engine began making unhappy noises. Soon, the bus slowed down and stopped in the middle of the road—an engine failure. While everyone scowled at the driver, my eyes remained fixated on the girl standing before the door, blocking the way. The bus journey had started only 10 minutes ago, so I had no idea what she would do when people had to get off. I was too busy capturing her beauty in my head to care, anyway. I struggled to get a good look with all the people crammed in the aisle. The way her hair swayed with the soft peaks of wind and the way she smiled when it did was mesmerizing. My mobile phone captured a hazy but good-enough picture of her and saved it. In the back of my head, I kept thinking of a killer starter line, but all I came up with was "Hey!" She looked carefree and relaxed, while I was growing nervous about talking to her. The surrounding people weren't getting any calmer, either. They kept shouting at the driver. Those of us standing in the aisle, like me, were irritated by the humidity and the turn of events. Her bewitching eyes darted here and there, trying to glimpse everything. I had to talk to her. I just had to.

After going over the carefully selected words again, I pushed people aside and made my way through the crowd. Angry words were thrown at me, but I only cared about the girl. My stumbling feet carried me to the door, and I locked my eyes—and my heart—on this young lady. She was gazing at the peonies outside, which swayed with the wind to match the cloudy weather. I noticed she wasn't at all bothered by the fact that the bus hadn't moved an inch in the last hour. Strange. But it also meant she was calm. Finally, I gathered the courage and said, "Hey!" A second later, when I realized what I'd said and the tone in which I'd said it, I wanted to punch myself in the face. I had kind of prepared a speech to start the conversation. Now, all the wonderful words that could've made me seem like an adept 19-year-old were lost. Anyway, the girl glanced at me. A second later, she went pale.

No words came out of her mouth. She just kept staring at me. Was she going to hit me? This thought had never crossed my mind before. What if she hit me in front of all these people? That would be the worst-case scenario. Or so I thought. "Hi," I said, this time trying to bring a curious gleam to my eyes to make myself seem less like a terrorist. Fear crossed her face as she gasped. "You shouldn't be able to see me..." It took me a while to digest what she had said. At first, it seemed like a joke. Then I noticed her expression seemed genuine—eyes wide with horror. Right then, a passenger lost his mind, scowled another two words at the helpless driver, and got off the bus. How? Well, he went right through the girl. The bright colors of the environment smudged into each other, while the distinct lines of the bus turned into blurry figures. A second later, the roof collapsed along with the bus itself. Bright colors scattered everywhere as everything went blurry. I felt a perplexing force hit me and knock me over. I fell into a dark abyss and screamed. Beep! Beep! Beep!

I woke up with a start. I had never had a dream so terrible. And now, I wanted to see that girl. The alarm clock was beeping furiously. I glanced at the time displayed on the window. 5:47 a.m. Or was it 6:47 a.m.? My vision was blurred, but I ignored it. The weather outside was windy and cloudy, although the weather app on my phone predicted a sunny day. On my desk sat my workstation computer, with a mess of wires spidering out to every corner of my room. Soft lights greeted me as I woke up. My neck was aching severely. As soon as I tried to stand, I lost my balance and hit the floor. I was frustrated. It took me quite a while to get back to normal. It felt as if someone were pulling the life out of me. Who was she? I reached for my diary and wrote down the details of this eerie dream sequence. It is scientifically proven that writing things down helps with memory. But I didn't want to remember the events. I just wanted to capture the girl in my memory.

There was no way. To remember the girl, I would have to remember the dream as well. I tied the laces on my shoes and prepared to step outside the house to lighten my mood. I slid down the stairs, trying not to make any noise and wake my parents. The door squeaked slightly as I left my residence. Ominous clouds hung overhead, casting an unsettling feel over the surroundings. On the other hand, the natural features of the town were vibrant. It felt as if heaven and hell had been intertwined. I arrived at the park, which had become one of my favorite places over the past few months, mainly because of the lush greenery and the calming atmosphere. I loved nature with all my soul. It helped me cope with my work.

Today, the ambiance of the parkland provided me with a platform to think deeply and resolve my problems. I slid out my phone to check for any new messages or emails. While reading an email from a friend, my finger slipped and hit the picture gallery app. The smartphone responded instantly, greeting me with a photo I had taken about an hour ago: a girl with flowing red hair, looking out through the windows of a bus. The same girl. I rubbed my eyes and stared at the picture again. Hazy, but good enough. It was the photo I had taken on the bus. Now I didn't need to remember the girl because my phone had captured her in its memory. I couldn't understand a thing. The world started spinning. I rushed home as quickly as possible and lay down on my bed, trying to forget everything. But no, I couldn't. That girl... Who was she? I had seen her in a dream. Then how did she appear on my smartphone? I had taken the photo, yes. But it was a dream! My questions to myself went unanswered, and so did my phone, a few hours later. I had passed out on the bed after returning from the park. I walked to my parents' room with a headache tearing at my insides.

It surprised them that I had slept again after my routine nature stroll. I hardly ever fell asleep after the walk. Something was wrong—I was sure of it. I moved to the living room and checked my phone again. To my surprise, the picture had disappeared. I practically turned my phone inside out looking for it. I searched everywhere—VNC servers, root memory, EEPROM, even the encrypted files on my phone and the cloud servers I had connected to. I found nothing. I called a friend of mine who had tried to reach me earlier when I passed out. She was also a tech enthusiast, so I asked her for help. "So, you had the picture in your so-called 'safe storage,' and after a few hours, it disappeared?" She spoke with a peculiar tone. I knew she'd target my poor storage system, but I also knew she'd have a solution. "Yes." "Upgrade your storage security, dude. Get some good servers!" "Yeah, I know, but I don't have the resources you do. For now, just stick to the point. I'm testing a new wireless cloud system at home." "Okay, give me access to the server, and I'll try." Her voice sounded geeky. After what felt like an eternity, a message popped up on my screen: "Found it." A picture was attached underneath.

I was relieved to get the picture back. I called Marzia again. She explained the possible security threats posed by my new server and told me the picture had been moved automatically due to some safety features. A sigh of relief escaped my throat. I had thought someone was trying to steal from my server. "Thanks for helping me out..." "Hey, wait. Who is this, by the way? I've never seen her before. Is she your new interest?" Marzia's voice turned playful by the time she reached the last line. "No, it's a long story. I'll tell you later. Bye..."

Two months passed in silence. Even after scouring every nook and corner of my memories, I couldn't place the girl. She was just in the picture. She was everywhere, yet she was nowhere. This search had turned into an obsession of mine. Meanwhile, I received a scholarship from an esteemed university. For higher studies, I had to relocate to another town, nestled at the foot of a mountain. Good for me, as I needed a change, anyway.

Today was moving day. I didn't have a lot of stuff, but packing it all was difficult. My room was still undone, with a massive spiderweb of wires stretched out in the middle of the space. Ironically, the wires that made all the tech stuff possible were the hardest to sort out. Some of my friends had come over to say goodbye. This house had given me most of my good memories—from my childhood to now, 19 years. That's a long time. I wondered if this house had any connection to the teenager from my dream. Nothing unusual had happened in the last two months. I had done everything I could to remember the exact location of where my fantasy had taken place. It was a hilly area, and the bus had broken down on one of the downhill roads. Peonies bloomed on the hillside, and greenery was a defining feature of that place. Finally, the girl. "You shouldn't be able to see me..." That sentence had changed how I thought about the sequences that unfold when you sleep. Somehow, I had a strong feeling I could find the girl in the real world—that we had a connection. Pushing these thoughts away, I turned back to the party my friends and family had organized. Of my two suitcases, one was filled with absolute geekery. My friends and family stayed with me until the very moment the train began to move.

My mom was in tears, and my dad looked proud. Some of my friends were sobbing, too! Even though everyone was in a sad mood, I was happy to be moving to a new place. Peace. It wasn't hard to leave it all behind. I was excited for a new beginning. I smiled at them through the window, knowing they would all miss me. As I relaxed in my seat, little did I know that I was embarking on a dangerous journey. In almost no time, I was set up in the new place. Everything was going fine. My new college was outstanding. People took an active interest in my technical skills. This town had hills I could explore, and a lot of greenery. Trees were everywhere. It felt almost like a movie—calm and subtle, the kind of ambiance perfect for daydreaming and, well, studying, since that's what I was there for. A few weeks passed, taking with them the newness of the place. Now, I had adjusted to everything, and frankly, I didn't want to return home.

I could never study inside, so I ventured outside to find a suitable place to calm my mind and focus on my books. About a hundred and fifty meters from my hostel was a large patch of elevated land. The canopy of this area was overwhelming. Behind the small forest was a waterfall! It was enough to be called an oasis. The pine tree, which usually provided cool shade while I studied, looked grumpy today. Its leaves swayed tremendously, even though strong winds hadn't greeted us in over a week. The other trees stayed still, as if they were all watching a show. The gentle swaying gradually turned into a powerful spin, forming a little tornado around the tree. I was shocked to witness such a phenomenon. Turning my attention to the base of the pine tree, I noticed a small figure. As I inched closer, my focus returned to the tree. The little tornado had become a massive one, reaching up to the clouds, as if connecting the tree with heaven. The person stood near the roots, as if all of this were child's play. Long hair swirled around the figure as the tornado grew stronger. It seemed as if it was draining the life from the tree. The person stood there, motionless.

By now, a thunderous, roaring storm had begun in the area. I shouted to grab the person's attention, but the wailing wind wouldn't let us communicate. Instinctively, I jumped into the black mass swirling around the trunk to save the person. I fell at her feet. She took a step back, fear creeping across her face. Her eyes widened as she glanced around. A teenage girl. Without saying a word, I grabbed her and jumped out of the rising black matter. We both hit the rough pavement with a thud. I had saved her.

As soon as we hit the ground, the tornado stopped swirling, as if someone had pressed a pause button on its life. Then something incredible happened. The winds began blowing in the opposite direction, effectively tearing through the dark mass and blowing it away. All the leaves and branches fell to the ground in an instant. This all happened within 10 seconds. Amazing. I turned toward the girl, but she had already walked off. She wasn't a normal girl. Then I realized something. She was the same girl. I checked the picture on my phone to verify. Indeed, she was the same girl.

I ran toward Central Square and found her crossing the road. A car, speeding along, appeared out of nowhere. But it was too late. She was going to be crushed. Yet, the car went right through her. The girl kept walking, as if nothing had happened. I ran toward her, eager to talk. The car passing through her had confirmed she was the one I had been searching for. The cars? I had almost forgotten that traffic was still coming my way. Their honks snapped me back to attention, and I quickly dodged them. At first, I was nervous about my decision, but instead of talking to her immediately, I followed her. She walked down the middle of the road, invisible to everyone else. Was she a ghost?

The mysterious girl kept walking. The street was nearly deserted, but she kept walking. I'm not sure why I decided to follow her, but it turned out to be a bad idea. After a while, the girl hissed, "Why are you following me?" That too, without looking back at me. I froze in place.

No words escaped my mouth. After a while, her pace quickened. She started walking downhill, toward an abandoned house, isolated from the rest of the town by thick foliage. The abandoned building had once been a lavish mansion, but now all that remained were enormous blocks of concrete. The sun, with its orange hues, began to set. The figure I was following kept walking along the faint trail in the grass.

"Hey! Will you stop?" The words finally came out. A mysterious aura lingered in the air as she walked. She stopped dead upon hearing my voice. For a moment, silence prevailed. Then she spoke in a shrill voice.

"You can see me, right?"

"Of course I can see you," I replied. The slight sarcasm in my voice was unintentional.

"You shouldn't be able to..." she said.

This activated a sense of déjà vu in my mind, and things finally clicked into place. Now I was sure this girl was the same person who had magically appeared in my sleep. I glanced at the mansion ruins and then at the dark sky. I felt like I was part of a horror movie.

I tried to focus all my attention on the mortal I was conversing with. Her auburn red hair reached all the way to her knees, engulfing her shoulders and most of her body along the way. It created a striking contrast with the bright green grass she walked on.

Suddenly, she turned to face me, not moving an inch in any direction, as if she had been petrified. A neutral expression followed. Another long pause. Her eyes, shining with a million hues of blue, captivated me. She was beautiful. Then came the realization: no one but me could see her.

"My name is Zeyra," she said. This time, the pause was on my side. I think my blood forgot how to circulate. I was too busy absorbing her unbelievable radiance. Then it clicked.

"Uhh... Hi... Zeyra..." What a precious name, I thought.

"You must think I'm a ghost or something, right?" She raised an eyebrow and leaned forward.

"I don't know, I haven't encountered a specter before," I replied. What I really meant to say was, "Yes, you're so beautiful, I thought of you as a ghost—too good to be true."

"You don't know..." , "Then let me explain".

"I am neither a phantom nor a mortal," she spoke quietly, her voice brittle. "When I was 15, some jealous gods punished me. They had some sort of competition, I think. I was told they had an unusual desire to be the most charming, even if no one could see them. I think they found me in their way and punished me." Her eyes welled up with tears. "I had done nothing wrong. They turned my ordinary life into a half-life, and now I have nothing to do here. I just roam around places I like, those I couldn't explore as a human."

The distance between us seemed to fade as she continued her story. "Ordinary people can't see me, but you can." At this, Zeyra's finger pointed at me. "Besides this, some gods live ordinary lives as humans. I am looking for them. Will you help me?"

I stood rock-still. Her words swirled in my head, and suddenly, they all fell into place. A smile curled across my lips. "Sure, I'll help you."

She was searching for her gods, seeking answers. Why had she been given a half-life? What would the gods say? They'd say they didn't want any mortal to be more charming than them, even if it didn't matter.

The gods are satisfied today, with only them shining the brightest. Her endless search doesn't matter. It doesn't matter because the more she searches for them, the harder it will be to find them. They possess improbable power at their fingertips, and yet humans like Zeyra find it safe to question them, probing to find what is right and what is wrong. She's looking for her gods, right? One of them is standing right in front of her. I've been the god in disguise. What happens now? Well, it's definitely not in her hands.

CHAPTER TWENTY-SIX

Cursed Valor

About the Author: Shlok Pandey

Born in Varanasi, Shlok Pandey is an 11th-grade student at Sunbeam Bhagwanpur with a passion for writing fantasy stories while exploring various genres. To date, he has penned three short stories. In addition to writing, he enjoys reading novels, watching movies, and playing various sports, making him a well-rounded enthusiast of storytelling and creativity.

*****

Chapter 1: Winter

The horse was dead. It was evident as it had stopped shivering. The world draped in white, the snowy hell! He had been on the mountain for a few hours or maybe a few days. The sun didn't seem to set on the mountain. He checked his arm again. He lifted the blood-stained sleeve. It was a terrifying sight that broke his will once more. His left arm was dark blue and rotten. He would have to cut it off, but where was the will? Still, it was the least of his worries. He had to get going.

He set off once more from the cave, which might have been the last one. He had to move because the horse was now too tough to cut. He had to find food, real food, and not the raw meat of rabbits. Perchance, he might find a descent. And so, he did. After walking for what felt like hours, perhaps longer, he found the fall. The mountain had been on a continuous rise the entire time he was on it. Luck was finally by his side.

There is always a descent to a mountain. It was not a piece of cake to descend. He likely broke a limb or two and maybe a few teeth as he fell ten to twenty times on the soft-hard snow. The snow gave way, gravel took over, and then the rocks paved the way for plains. Before long, he found himself half-dead on a green patch, gasping for air, each breath more labored than the last.

As soon as he heard the splashing and rush of water, he looked around desperately. He then realized there was a waterfall just ahead as the mountain took a curve. Out of thirst, he crawled with all the might he could muster toward the quick river. He felt the sharpest pain he had ever felt whenever he moved even an inch. The world trembled around him as his fingers dipped into the icy water. His hand, shaking from exhaustion, scooped a handful to his parched lips. As the water slid down his throat, his eyes shut.

"Oh dear lord, he woke up!"

"No, he hasn't... oh yes, he has."

His drowsy eyes were still half-shut, but his ears were awake. He could sense a bunch of people gathered around him. He woke with a start.

"Huh? Where am I? God Ho! Who are you all? And where is my hor..."

And then he remembered.

"Ay, are yeh a warrior or something?" said a queer voice.

"Yes! I uh... yes, I am." His head was hurting—a sharp, piercing pain that wouldn't go away.

"A warrior, you say? You look more like a ghost," the queer voice replied with even more skepticism.

"I want... can I have some water?" His voice cracked as his head throbbed.

"You need something more than just water. Have you come down from the mountains?" said the sweet, soothing voice of a pretty countrywoman, as his eyes could see by then.

"By all the great lands, yes."

"Then we might have some medicine for you. You are facing seasonal change."

Chapter 2: Witch

The time flew by as the warrior spent his days in the village. He became good friends with the soothing woman, whose name was Rose. The middle-aged, skeptical man too became one of his allies, fascinated by his build. He had called him 'a strong man' quite a few times. As for his hands, the villagers weren't bothered; they had seen much worse. Still, the cure they suggested was painful.

A few more peaceful days passed without disturbance, until a young man approached him. The man was tall and skinny, with a beard and a confident stride.

"A fine day, sir."

"Absolutely."

"Sir, may I ask you for a favor?" His voice was sweet.

"Go on, I'm all ears," the warrior replied, already expecting something like this.

"Do you know about the witch of the waterfall?"

"If there were a witch, I would not be standing here."

"She lives on the other side, my lord."

"Oh, I see... you want me to finish her."

"Yes, my lord. By the heavens, she deserves to die. She has committed sins beyond one's imagination."

"All right, all right, I don't want to hear about them. I'll go as soon as I'm fit. Almost there now," he said, believing he could manage something even with his dried arm. After all, it had to be a weakling; all the strong ones had died during the time of Pitch, the strongest wizard who was said to be the kindest of all the wizards and witches.

At the brink of dawn, the warrior left the wooden, most beautiful village amidst gasps, optimism, and smiles. Rose, along with a few others, was deeply worried about his safe return, but he assured her. He made the promise of never coming back until the witch was slain.

Splat!

As soon as he reached the witch's dwelling, something hard as a rock fell on him. It broke on impact, revealing a strange, solid-liquid. As he looked up, he was mesmerized. Eggs were raining from the sky—hundreds of them, all at once. It was the most magnificent magic he had ever witnessed.

The eggs continued to rain, splattering around as he wandered in search of the hut. The warrior wiped the strange, glowing liquid from his armor, a part of him still caught in the enchantment of it all. But he couldn't let himself be swayed. He took a deep breath and stepped forward, gripping the hilt of his sword as he finally found something that looked like a witch's hut.

The door was neither enchanted nor locked. This struck him as strange.

"What brings you here, dear?" came a hoarse voice.

She appeared from behind a curtain leading west to another room. He caught a glimpse of the room—bones on a table, potions scattered across what seemed like a large workbench. Her eyes were blood-red. She was not like other witches; there was something about her, something that made her stronger, though he had no idea what it was.

Whatever the case, he wasn't ready to fight her. Then he remembered his promise, but his conscious mind sidelined it as a mere thought. His voice trembled as he spoke.

"I am in trouble, my great lady. I am here asking for some aid. You see, my hand..." He showed her his hand, hoping she might have some compassion.

But she started to laugh.

"Oh, I am sorry. You see, I wanted a hand like yours for my next potion. None of the bones I gathered from the mountain had these peculiar frostbite remains. The stars align, dear heavens."

"So, you have my hand, and let me have some aid," he said, scared and wanting no trouble.

"You will. Haha. You definitely will." Her eyes glowed ominously.

The pact was made. In return for his hand, the witch provided him with fine white armor, adorned with gold lines and a bold green cape. She replaced his left arm with a strange black contraption shaped like a hand. He wished it worked, but he didn't dare to ask for more, afraid of angering her. He thought he might bring stronger warriors to her place later.

"Bless you," she said cheerfully.

"I thank you, my lady."

Her smile suddenly vanished, and her eyes glowed again, this time ferociously.

"Let me tell you, you dare not reveal my dwelling to anyone. Or this armor will crush you."

The warrior nodded. He had anticipated something like this. She smiled again.

"Might I ask why the eggs were raining?" he said, trying to change the topic.

She replied, "The spell misfired again! I was boiling eggs!"

Chapter 3: Wisdom

He returned to the village, which rejoiced at the arrival of the great warrior who had slain the witch of the waterfall. But they could see a change in his behavior and appearance. There was something off about him that surprised everyone.

Ignoring everyone, including Rose, he went straight to the young man. Without a word, he drew his sword and stabbed him in the stomach so harshly that the blade went all the way through.

Gasps filled the air. Shock and fear gripped the villagers as they stood frozen, unable to speak. The warrior, without hesitation, turned and dashed away, his steps swift as he ran through the winds and out of the village.

He made his way back toward the waterfall, his mind in turmoil. There, under a large oak tree, he saw an old man sitting and calmly smoking tobacco.

"Why did I come to you? And WHAT HAVE I DONE?!" he screamed, his voice filled with anguish.

The old man replied softly, "You have come to me because I called you. And you, my boy, have committed a sin—an unforgivable sin."

The warrior fell to his knees, his eyes brimming with sorrow. "It's the witch's magic," he murmured, his voice cracking.

The old man took a long puff of his pipe before continuing. "Anger flushes out the dignity of a man, and you, my boy, have chosen anger and fear as your allies—or, I should say, your greatest enemies."

The warrior's voice trembled. "How... how can I fix it?"

The old man extended a small dagger toward him. "Here, take this. This will help you."

Epilogue

He knew what he had to do now. He reached the witch's den once again, this time for the final confrontation.

The witch was outside this time. She turned to him with a curious look. "What happened?"

"I am here to kill you, and I will fulfill the promise I made," he said, his voice steady.

She chuckled darkly. "Haha, you are funny."

"I am not joking, all right," he replied, drawing his sword from its sheath.

Her expression faltered for a moment, but then her laughter grew louder. "You think you can?"

Her laughter stopped abruptly, and her face twisted in fury. Her eyes began to glow, black as pitch. She was more than just angry now.

He charged at her, lifting his sword high. But she caught it midair with her bare hands. Not a single drop of blood emerged from her body. She smiled, a wicked grin spreading across her face.

And then, he remembered. He knew what he was meant to do.

With a swift motion, he pulled out the dagger and slashed her from abdomen to jaw in one clean motion. Blood poured in torrents, but it wasn't just blood. From the wound, a black flame erupted, snaking into the air and entering his nostrils as he inhaled.

They both fell to the ground.

The warrior woke as dusk settled over the land, bathing the world in a golden hue. The landscape, though eerily quiet, looked more beautiful than he had ever seen it.

His head spun as he staggered to his feet. He walked to the waterfall and bent down to wash his face. As his hands cupped the water, his reflection stared back at him. His eyes—they were darker now, much like those of Pitch, the dead wizard.

He returned to the witch, who lay motionless on the ground. He leaned over her, watching for any sign of life.

She was dead. It was evident—she had stopped shivering.

CHAPTER TWENTY-SEVEN

A Nameless Girl

About the Author: Shriya Singh Chauhan
Shriya is a current student with a passion for reading and writing in her free time. She enjoys crafting both poetry and short stories, often drawing inspiration from her favorite authors, Agatha Christie and Edgar Allan Poe. While she primarily writes in the fantasy genre, she believes that a touch of thriller adds an exciting twist to her narratives.

*****

Drip ... surgical lights illuminated the sterile room.

Drip ... IV fluids trickled into veins.

Drip ... resuscitation attempts echoed in the room.

Drip ... a flatline pierced through the cold silence.

An Hour Earlier

The screech of failed brakes tore through the highway. Headlights swerved, blinding the night. Her screams—sharp and desperate—were swallowed by the roar of metal twisting against metal. A sickening crunch, then silence. She lay there, bleeding profusely, her head resting against shattered glass. Her once delicate white sundress was now a gruesome canvas of crimson. Broken bones jutted awkwardly, her arm at an unnatural angle. She was lifeless, but the paramedics refused to give up.

Now

The girl was rushed into the hospital, her stretcher leaving a trail of blood that stained the pristine white tiles. She was a Jane Doe—no ID, no name, no one looking for her. Just a girl in her late teens, clinging to the frayed edge of life.

The doctors worked tirelessly, their faces taut with concentration. They tried everything—suturing the deep gash on her head, stabilizing her shattered bones, infusing blood to replace what she'd lost. But hour after hour, her heartbeat waned until it disappeared entirely. Her lifeless body rested as the medical team covered her face with a sterile sheet.

At the exact moment the monitor displayed a flatline, another room in the hospital erupted with noise.

An IV dripped rhythmically beside another patient's bed—a seventeen-year-old girl who had been in a coma for two years. Cynthia. Her parents kept vigil every day, praying for a miracle that never came.

Until now.

"Her eyes!" her mother screamed. "She's waking up! Call the doctors! Someone, please!"

The doctors, abandoning their failed attempt to revive the nameless girl, rushed to Cynthia's room. The sight of her fluttering eyelids drew gasps of astonishment.

"Is this real? Is she awake?" her father stammered.

"Where ... am I?" Cynthia murmured weakly.

"Ceecee, sweetheart, it's alright. You're going to be alright," her mother said, her voice trembling as tears streamed down her face.

"Ceecee?" Cynthia echoed, sitting up slowly.

"Ms. Cynthia," the doctor interrupted, stepping forward. "How are you feeling? Any headaches? Trouble seeing?"

Cynthia's brow furrowed. "Who ... who's Cynthia?"

Silence thickened the air.

"Run the bloodwork and schedule an MRI," the doctor ordered swiftly, ushering everyone out of the room.

"What do you mean she doesn't remember her name?" Cynthia's father demanded, his voice frantic.

The doctor spoke with careful precision. "We can't draw any conclusions yet. For now, try to keep her calm. Let us handle the questions."

Hours later, the scans revealed an inexplicable truth—Cynthia had suffered damage to her temporal lobe while unconscious. She remembered nothing—not her name, her parents, or the accident that put her in the coma. She drifted into sleep, exhausted from the endless questions.

The Dream

She found herself standing on the porch of a quaint lakeside house, its reflection shimmering in the still water. The air smelled of earth and fresh blooms. Drawn to the garden, she walked toward the ivy-covered swing, where someone sat, tearing leaves apart.

It was herself—or someone who looked just like her.

"Hello, Ariadne," the doppelgänger greeted, patting the swing beside her.

"Ariadne?" she asked, sitting down hesitantly.

"That's your name," the other said, shredding another leaf.

"And who are you?"

"Cynthia, of course." The doppelgänger plucked a daisy from the overgrown grass.

"How do you know my name is Ariadne?"

"Because I need you," Cynthia replied softly. "And you need me. I need you to take my place. Have a second chance at life—for I can't go on much longer. Give my parents the daughter they've been waiting for."

"But everyone's been calling me Cynthia," Ariadne said.

"And so will you. Once you wake up, my memories will be yours. That is all you'll remember."

Cynthia handed Ariadne the daisy and covered her hand with her own. A sharp pain burned through Ariadne's palm as though acid seared her skin.

Awake

She woke with a start.

"Ceecee, are you alright?" her mother asked anxiously.

"Yes," she replied, her voice steadier than before. "Mum, Dad ... can we go home?"

The doctors, baffled by the miraculous recovery, allowed her to leave. Somehow, her temporal lobe had healed completely.

The Ride Home

In the car, 'Cynthia' stared out the window, watching grey clouds drift across the sky. Her parents chatted softly in the front seats, occasionally glancing back at her with relief and gratitude.

She glanced at her palm, tracing the daisy-shaped scar that now adorned it. Her lips curled into a faint smile—not of joy, but of understanding. She wasn't Cynthia, not truly.

But for the sake of those who loved her, she would become her.

CHAPTER TWENTY-EIGHT

A Soul Trapped

About the Author: Sunaina Singh Kashyap
Born into a loving family, I enjoyed a wonderful childhood filled with laughter. Passionate about swimming and basketball, I earned medals while forming lasting friendships along the way. Now, as a 12th grader, I am pursuing engineering, driven by curiosity and a desire to excel. The pandemic sparked my interest in IT engineering, and with a strong foundation in the field, I am committed to tackling challenges and making a meaningful impact. I am grateful to my parents for their unwavering support and am eager for what the future holds.

*****

I still remember that evening vividly. My grandmother had gathered us—her grandchildren—around her. We were playing, laughing, and teasing our youngest cousin when someone casually said, "Are you out of your mind?" in a playful tone. It felt harmless at the time.

But my grandmother's expression shifted. She grew serious, and the laughter around us faded. She looked at us, and with a sigh, began sharing a story that would leave a lasting impression on me.

"Abha," she began, "your distant aunt, was born with unique challenges. She had autism and struggled with certain aspects of life. Her parents, out of love, never sought help for her. They hoped she could live a normal life like everyone else. When the time came, they married her to a good family, believing it would bring her happiness and stability."

She paused, her tone tinged with sadness. "But things didn't go as they had hoped. Abha's husband and his family didn't understand her. They made fun of her innocence and took advantage of her trust. She stayed with them for a while, but eventually, they sent her back to her parents, taking her jewelry and belongings but leaving behind her shattered dreams."

We listened quietly as Grandma continued. "Her husband remarried and built a new life. Years later, his child from the second marriage, now a successful engineer, learned about Abha's story. Unlike his father, he showed kindness and respect when he met her. Those moments of dignity meant a lot to Abha, even though they came late."

Her voice softened as she went on. "Abha's brothers, though, could have done more. They cared for her in their way but saw her as a responsibility rather than a part of the family. They gave her a room in the house, but it wasn't what you'd call welcoming. Some neighbors visited her out of kindness, but most people avoided her, thinking she was strange. It wasn't cruelty, exactly, but there was a lack of understanding and compassion."

My grandmother sighed deeply. "Even so, Abha never stopped hoping. Every time the phone rang, she would get excited, thinking it was her husband calling. She'd tell the younger kids, 'See, my husband has called!' But, of course, it was never him. He eventually felt regret for how he treated her, but it came too late to make a difference in her life."

She paused, looking at us with kind but firm eyes. "Abha's story is a lesson," she said. "It's a reminder of how important it is to treat everyone with love and respect, no matter what challenges they face. Even small acts of kindness can mean the world to someone. Words, too, carry weight. What seems like a joke to us can hurt someone more deeply than we realize."

That evening, her words stayed with me. It made me think about how casually we use words like "mad" or "crazy" without considering their impact. Abha's story wasn't just about her struggles; it was about the importance of humanity, acceptance, and understanding.

I learned that being compassionate and kind isn't just about grand gestures—it's about the small things, the words we use, the care we show, and the effort we make to understand others. Because, at the end of the day, humanity is what makes life meaningful.

CHAPTER TWENTY-NINE

The Neck Hunter

About the Author: Suryank Raj
Suryank is a seventeen-year-old student in Class 12 at Sunbeam English School in Bhagwanpur, Varanasi. While he has a talent for writing songs and rap, he is a fresh voice in the world of storytelling. With a burgeoning interest in the thriller, mystery, and horror genres, Suryank is eager to explore new styles to enhance his writing skills.

*****

It's often said that villains are made, not born. But sometimes, the road to redemption is paved with scars—and the ghosts of unanswered questions.

In the early 2000s, Chicago was alive with the hum of a bustling city. Beneath its towering skyscrapers and crowded streets lived a boy named William. To the world, he was invisible. At home, his father's anger filled the air like a storm waiting to break, and his mother's fragile attempts to protect him only made her a target. At school, William wasn't much luckier. Laughter wasn't something he shared in—it was something hurled at him, sharp and cruel. Teachers noticed the bruises but stayed silent.

As he grew older, the wounds of his childhood didn't fade. They hardened into a shell of distrust and simmering anger. William kept to himself, working at a garage where greasy tools and the smell of oil became his only company. He spoke little, kept his head down, but inside, his pain churned like a volcano waiting to erupt.

One cold night, under the yellow glow of streetlights, it finally did. A group of men cornered him, mocking his silence, pushing him, laughing. One shove too many was all it took. William grabbed a stick and lashed out. When the chaos settled, one man lay motionless on the ground, blood spreading beneath him. The sound of distant sirens froze William in place, and for the first time in his life, he felt something other than fear. He felt power.

The court called it manslaughter. William was sentenced to five years in prison, where survival became his new reality. Guilt didn't follow him behind bars—not in the way most would expect. To William, he hadn't taken a life; he had fought for his own.

When he was released, William wanted to start fresh. He moved to a new city and took a quiet job at a small bookstore. Among the dusty shelves, he found a fragile peace. The solitude felt safe. For a while, it was enough.

But peace doesn't last.

One afternoon, as he stacked books, he noticed a little girl sitting cross-legged on the floor, reading. Her laughter broke through the silence like sunlight piercing a dark room. Something about her stirred a memory deep within him—a glimpse of innocence he thought he'd lost forever.

When he approached her, she looked up with wide, knowing eyes. "You're not supposed to be here," she said softly. Then, before he could respond, she bolted out the door. Left behind was a single daisy, tucked into the spine of her book. William picked it up, feeling an unease he couldn't explain.

That night, his dreams took a dark turn. He saw a massive wooden door carved with faces—some crying, some smiling. Beyond it was a dimly lit room. A swing draped in ivy hung in the center, and on it sat a man whose face felt eerily familiar.

"Hello, William," the man said, his voice calm yet chilling.

"Who are you?" William asked, his heart pounding.

The man leaned forward, his smile thin and unsettling. "Someone who knows your pain—and your secrets."

"What secrets?" William whispered, his throat tight.

The man's voice turned sharp. "Do you really think that night was an accident? That your rage was entirely your own?"

William woke in a cold sweat, his palm stinging. When he turned on the light, he saw it—a fresh scar in the shape of a daisy.

In the weeks that followed, strange things began to happen. An envelope arrived at the bookstore with no return address. Inside was a photograph of the man he had killed years ago. His face was intact, but his eyes had been scratched out. On the back, a note read: "You took him from us. Now we take you."

Then, another body was found—the first of the men who had fled the alley that night. Clutched in his lifeless hand was a daisy.

As the bodies piled up, William's nightmares grew darker. Voices haunted him, whispering accusations. "You thought you were free, but the past never stays buried."

Digging through old police records, William uncovered a terrifying truth. The man he had killed wasn't just another thug. He was the younger brother of a powerful crime lord who had disappeared after William's trial. The daisy scar on his palm wasn't a coincidence. It was a message—a mark that his life would unravel, one piece at a time.

The little girl wasn't who he thought she was, either. At first, he believed she was connected to one of the men from that fateful night. But as he dug deeper, he discovered the impossible: she was his niece. A sister he thought he'd lost to foster care had grown up, had a child, and somehow found her way back into his life.

The man from his dreams wasn't just a figment of his imagination, either. He was real—a childhood friend turned enemy, pulling strings from the shadows, using guilt and manipulation to destroy William's fragile new life.

In the end, it all came to a head in the bookstore's basement. William stood face to face with his old friend, the truth unraveling between them like a thread pulled too far. The air was thick with dust and the metallic tang of blood, the silence broken only by their ragged breaths.

"You could've stopped this," his friend whispered, a faint smile curling his lips despite the pain. "But you didn't. You let it all happen."

William's hands trembled, his fist clenching the daisy scar that burned like an unspoken condemnation. "You wanted me to suffer," he said quietly, his voice raw with anger and grief. "You twisted everything—made me the villain."

His friend laughed weakly. "Aren't you?"

The sirens grew louder, their wail cutting through the stillness. As the red and blue lights flickered through the cracks of the basement window, William realized the weight of what he'd done. The past he'd tried to bury had come back, dragging him down like quicksand.

When the police arrived, William was standing over the lifeless body, his shoulders slumped. The daisy scar on his palm throbbed like a curse, a reminder of everything he'd lost—his innocence, his peace, his second chance at life.

But as the officers moved closer, William made a decision. He raised his hands, the scar exposed under the dim light, and let them take him. There would be no running, no more hiding from the truth.

In the days that followed, the story spread like wildfire. To the world, William became many things—a killer, a victim, a man haunted by his past. Yet in the quiet of his cell, he found something unexpected: clarity. The daisy on his palm no longer felt like a curse but a reminder of the life he could still rebuild, even from the ashes.

Some stories end with redemption. Others, like William's, end with reckoning.

Because sometimes, villains aren't born—they're forged in the fires of pain and loss. But even in the darkest places, a seed of hope can bloom.

CHAPTER THIRTY

Photographing Destiny

About the Author: Utkarsh

My name is Utkarsh, and I am an 11th-grade student. I would describe myself with words like multipotentialite, esoteric, autophile, introverted yet not shy, rational, polymath, cool, and perhaps a bit quirky. It's challenging to confine me to just a few labels, as I have a wide array of interests and hobbies. I enjoy traveling, writing, singing, debating, and cooking, and I have a genuine love for people. My ambition is to become a psychologist one day.

*****

At the edge of town, tucked away beneath the shadow of a weathered brick building, stood an unassuming photo booth. Its peeling red paint and rusting exterior gave it the air of a relic from a forgotten era. Yet, despite its decrepit appearance, this booth was anything but forgotten. Its legend had traveled far and wide: step inside, and the picture it prints won't be of you, but of your soulmate. In every tale, the booth had never been wrong.

No one knew its origin or how it worked. Despite its antiquated look, it never ran out of paper or ink. People had tried to dismantle it, to uncover its secrets, but each attempt ended the same way: the booth would vanish, only to resurface in a new corner of the world, waiting patiently for the next seeker.

Dylan had heard all the stories. Friends, cousins, even his neighbor had tried it. He'd seen the evidence himself—a neighbor proudly displaying a photo of her now-fiancé, grinning with unmistakable joy. While the skeptics in town dismissed the booth as a parlor trick, its accuracy was hard to ignore. Dylan had always brushed it off, but curiosity lingered. The idea of soulmates felt too neat, too fantastical. And yet, something about the mystery drew him in. Perhaps it was the whispers of hope that, somewhere out there, someone was meant for him.

On a crisp autumn morning, Dylan found himself standing at the end of the line. The booth had reappeared a few days ago, drawing a crowd of hopefuls, skeptics, and wide-eyed spectators. People shuffled forward one by one, their whispers mingling with the rustle of falling leaves. Some emerged from the booth with radiant smiles; others clutched their photos with looks of confusion, or even tear-streaked disbelief.

Dylan's turn arrived. He hesitated before stepping through the faded curtain.

Inside, the booth was cramped, the air faintly scented with old paper and timeworn machinery. The stool wobbled slightly as he sat down, staring at his own uncertain reflection in the polished glass of the lens. The weight of countless stories pressed on his chest. What if it was true? What if the picture really revealed the face of someone destined to change his life?

"Alright," he muttered to himself, shaking his head as if to dispel the growing nerves. "Let's get this over with."

He slid a coin into the slot. The machine whirred to life, the sound reverberating in the quiet space. A small screen flickered on, displaying a countdown: three, two, one. A blinding flash enveloped the tiny booth.

Moments later, the printer hummed, spitting out a glossy photo. Dylan's hand trembled as he reached for it, his heart pounding like a drum. The photo's surface was warm against his fingertips, the faint chemical scent of ink hanging in the air.

He turned it over.

And his heart stopped.

Dylan stared at the screen, his breath caught in his throat. The photo on the monitor was unmistakably her—the same long dark hair, the same piercing eyes. But the name and details didn't make sense.

"Lila Hartman?" Dylan whispered.

Andrew nodded, his brow furrowed in confusion. "Yeah. She went missing twenty years ago from a small town about three hours from here. The case went cold—no leads, no suspects. But this..." He gestured to the picture. "This is her. Or what she's supposed to look like now."

Dylan's mind raced. Twenty years? Missing? None of it added up. How could the booth have given him her picture if she wasn't even... He stopped himself, not daring to finish the thought.

"What happens now?" Dylan asked, his voice shaky.

Andrew leaned back in his chair, his eyes narrowing as he considered. "We reopen the case. I'll contact the detectives who worked on it, see if this leads to anything. But Dylan..." He hesitated. "If this photo is accurate, and she's still alive, we're dealing with something strange here. People don't just vanish for decades without a trace. There's a story behind this, and it's probably not a happy one."

Dylan nodded numbly, his fingers clutching the edge of the desk. He couldn't shake the feeling that he was now tangled in something far bigger than himself.

As he walked home, the photo burned in his pocket like a live ember. He replayed Andrew's words over and over: *missing for twenty years.* Yet the booth had chosen her. Why? Was she still alive? Was he meant to find her and somehow bring her home?

The next few weeks were a blur of waiting and wondering. Andrew kept him updated, but the leads were sparse. Lila's family had long since moved away, and most of the original investigators were retired. Still, Andrew assured him that the case was gaining traction.

Then, one evening, Dylan's phone rang. It was Andrew.

"We've got something," Andrew said, his voice tense. "A possible sighting."

Dylan's pulse quickened. "Where?"

"Small town, about an hour from here. A woman matching her description was seen working at a diner. The witness says she keeps to herself, doesn't talk much. But here's the thing—the name she's using? Lila."

Dylan's heart raced. "It has to be her."

"I'm not saying it is," Andrew cautioned. "But it's worth checking out. You want to come with me?"

"Yes," Dylan said without hesitation.

The drive felt endless, the miles stretching out under the weight of anticipation. When they arrived, the diner was nearly empty, its neon sign flickering against the twilight sky.

Andrew and Dylan stepped inside. A woman was wiping down the counter, her back to them. Dylan's breath hitched. Even from behind, he could tell it was her.

"Excuse me," Andrew said gently, stepping forward.

The woman turned, and Dylan felt the air leave his lungs. It was her. Older than the photo, but unmistakably the same person. Her eyes widened in recognition—or was it fear?

"Lila?" Andrew asked softly.

She froze, her knuckles white against the rag she was holding.

"I..." she stammered, her voice barely a whisper. "I don't know that name."

But Dylan knew it was her. He could feel it in his bones.

"Please," he said, stepping forward. He held out the photo, his hands trembling. "It's you. I've been looking for you."

Her eyes darted to the picture, then back to Dylan. Something shifted in her expression—fear giving way to something deeper.

"I don't understand," she whispered, tears welling in her eyes. "How did you find me?"

Dylan glanced at Andrew, then back at her. The words caught in his throat, but he knew they needed to be said.

"I think," he began, his voice soft but steady, "we were meant to find each other."

Lila hesitated, and Dylan could hear the weight of her breath on the other end of the line. "He's gone," she finally said, her voice heavy with a mix of relief and sorrow. "He passed away a few months ago. Heart attack."

Dylan's thoughts swirled. This revelation only deepened the mystery. "And that's when you decided to reach out? To leave?"

"Yes," Lila admitted. "After he died, I found... things. Documents, photos, pieces of the life I was supposed to have. It was overwhelming. But then, I saw something about the booth."

"The photo booth?" Dylan asked, leaning forward, his heart racing.

"Yes. My father had a file on it, like he was obsessed. He called it the 'soul window.' I don't know how, but he knew about its connection to people—how it works. I found an old article he had clipped, one of the first reports about it. He must have known I'd try to find the truth someday. And that's when I decided to let it find you."

Dylan's head spun. The booth wasn't just a mystical oddity—it had somehow been tied to her life, maybe even her father's paranoia. "You mean... you sent the picture to me?"

"Not exactly," Lila said softly. "The booth chooses. But I left it there, knowing that if it worked, it would bring me closer to someone who could help me—someone I could trust. And here you are."

Dylan's chest tightened. He had been drawn into her life by the booth's inexplicable magic, but now, the mystery was far more human—and far more dangerous.

"I need to see you," Dylan said, his voice firm. "I want to help you, Lila. I think I'm supposed to."

There was a long silence on the other end of the line. Finally, Lila spoke, her voice trembling. "Meet me tomorrow, just outside of town. There's an old bridge near Maple Creek. I'll explain everything."

Dylan's heart raced. "I'll be there."

The call ended, and Dylan sat in silence, the photo still clutched in his hand. This wasn't just about soulmates or destiny anymore. Lila's story was tangled in something dark and unresolved, and now, he was a part of it.

The next day, as the sun dipped low on the horizon, Dylan found himself standing by the bridge. The wind whispered through the trees, and the creek babbled softly below. He scanned the area, his nerves jangling.

Then, he saw her.

Lila emerged from the shadows, her figure framed by the golden light of the setting sun. She was just as beautiful as in the photo, but there was a weight in her eyes that no picture could capture—a lifetime of secrets and pain.

"Lila," Dylan said softly.

She gave him a tentative smile, and for a moment, the world seemed to pause. "Dylan," she replied.

As they stood there, the distance between them shrinking, Dylan realized that meeting her wasn't the end of the mystery—it was just the beginning.

"Tell me everything," he said, his voice steady.

And so, Lila began to unravel her story, the truth spilling out in pieces like shattered glass.

Would you like to continue from here, explore more of Lila's past, or delve into the connection between her father and the photo booth?

Dylan stepped inside, his heart thudding in his chest. The room was dimly lit, the air heavy with the scent of stale smoke and cheap cleaning products. It looked like it hadn't seen a proper cleaning in years—faded curtains hanging limply at the window, a threadbare carpet beneath their feet, and an old, creaky bed with a single lamp casting long shadows on the walls. Yet none of it mattered. All Dylan could focus on was Lila, standing in the center of the room, her eyes never leaving him.

She gestured toward a chair near the small, cracked table in the corner. "I didn't expect you to come so quickly," she said softly, almost as if apologizing.

Dylan sat down, his gaze never leaving her. "I told you I'd be here," he replied, his voice gentle, but with an undercurrent of determination. He didn't know what he was doing, what the next steps were, but somehow, being here with her felt like the only thing that mattered.

Lila took a seat across from him, her hands folded in her lap, her fingers trembling slightly. She looked vulnerable in a way Dylan had never seen before—a woman who had spent her entire life hidden away, afraid to trust anyone, to let anyone in. The walls she had built around herself were still there, but something in her eyes told him she wanted to let them come down, even if it scared her.

"I don't know what to say," Lila whispered, her voice shaking with emotion. "I don't even know who I am anymore." Her eyes welled with tears, but she blinked them away quickly, as if ashamed of the vulnerability.

Dylan leaned forward, his voice steady but full of empathy. "You're still you. No matter what's happened, no matter how much time has passed, you're still the same person. And you don't have to go through this alone anymore."

For the first time since they had met, a small flicker of hope seemed to stir in Lila's eyes. She wiped her cheek with the back of her hand, then took a deep breath. "I don't know how to live in the world anymore. It feels so... so foreign to me. Everything's changed."

Dylan nodded, understanding more than she might have realized. "The world has changed for all of us. But you're here now. You don't have to face it alone. You have me." He gave her a reassuring smile, though he wasn't entirely sure what he was offering, only that he wanted to help her in any way he could.

Lila's gaze softened, and for the briefest moment, Dylan saw a flicker of something—trust, maybe, or the beginning of acceptance. But then, just as quickly, the walls seemed to go back up. She leaned back in her chair, folding her arms across her chest, as if trying to protect herself from the world.

"I don't even know how to begin. I've spent so long hiding from everything—my father, the past, even myself. And now... now I'm supposed to just start over?"

Dylan reached out, his hand hovering near hers, not quite touching, but offering support nonetheless. "You don't have to start over right now. You can take it one step at a time. We'll figure it out together."

Lila looked down at the photo still clutched in Dylan's hand. "I don't understand why it was you. I thought... I thought soulmates were supposed to be this perfect thing, this magical connection. But I don't feel that magic. I don't feel anything like I'm supposed to."

Dylan hesitated, his heart heavy with the weight of her words. He wasn't sure how to respond. The connection between them felt real—he could see it in the way they spoke, in the way their lives had intersected in such an uncanny way. But he didn't have all the answers, and maybe neither did she.

"I don't know what this is either," he said softly, his voice earnest. "But I do know that you're here now. And maybe that's the beginning of something, even if it's not what we expected."

Lila met his gaze, her eyes searching his face for sincerity, for understanding. After a long silence, she nodded, just slightly, her shoulders relaxing. "Maybe. Maybe it's time to stop hiding."

For the first time since he'd walked into the room, Dylan felt a sense of calm. He couldn't fix everything, couldn't erase the past, but he could be here for her now. And maybe that was all they needed for the moment.

The two of them sat in silence for a while longer, the weight of their unspoken thoughts hanging in the air. Dylan could feel the rawness of Lila's pain, but also the quiet strength in her—a strength that had kept her going all these years, even when she didn't know if she could.

And for the first time in a long time, Dylan felt something stirring in his own heart: not just for Lila, but for what they might become, together, in this strange new world that neither of them quite understood yet.

Dylan felt a cold sweat break out on his skin as his mind raced. He couldn't tear his eyes away from the photo. It was him, standing frozen in time, staring back at him with the same intensity that had gripped him when he first saw Lila's face in the booth. But this was different. This wasn't just a picture. It felt like a warning.

Lila's hand hovered over the photo, but she couldn't bring herself to touch it again. "This... this isn't possible," she whispered, her voice strained with panic. "How... how did it get here?"

Dylan's heart was pounding so loudly he could barely hear his own thoughts. The booth. It had been the catalyst, the mysterious force that had brought them together, but now it seemed to be playing some cruel game with their lives. Why him? Why now?

"I don't know," Dylan managed, his voice tight. He reached out, fingers trembling as they brushed against the glossy surface of the photo. It felt warm, almost alive in his hand, as if it had just been printed moments ago. "But it's real. It's me."

Lila backed away, her face pale and stricken with fear. "The booth gave me your picture... and now it's giving you mine." Her voice quivered. "Do you think... do you think we're still supposed to be together? Is that what this means?"

Dylan swallowed hard, trying to shake off the sense of dread settling over him. He hadn't considered that. He had been so consumed by the thought of finding her, of understanding their connection, that he hadn't allowed himself to consider the darker implications of this whole situation.

"I don't know," he admitted, feeling a weight settle in his chest. "But this doesn't feel like a coincidence anymore. I think... I think there's something more happening here. Something bigger than us."

Lila's eyes darted around the room as if she expected something to leap out from the shadows. "What if it's not about us? What if it's about the booth? What if it's controlling us? Maybe we're just pawns in its game."

Dylan clenched his fists, his mind racing with the possibilities. Was the booth truly orchestrating their lives? Had it led him here for a reason—just to watch as everything spiraled into chaos?

Before he could speak, a voice crackled through the silence. Not from the phone, but from somewhere else—somewhere deeper. It sounded distant, distorted, but unmistakably familiar.

"Dylan."

"You hear that?" she whispered.

Dylan nodded slowly, his heart pounding. The sound was coming from the nightstand beside the bed, where Lila had placed a small, faded box. He hadn't noticed it before, but now it seemed out of place—too new, too clean for the room's dilapidated state.

Lila stood up, her hands trembling as she reached for the box. "It wasn't here when I checked in. I found it on the doorstep this morning... I thought it was just junk."

Before Dylan could stop her, she opened the lid. Inside was a single, glossy photo.

Dylan's blood ran cold as he stared at it.

It was him. His own face stared back at him from the photo—the same way Lila's had in the booth.

Lila's voice shook. "The booth... it's not done with us."
They both stared at the photo in stunned silence, the air around them thick with a sense of foreboding. Whatever they had thought they knew, whatever Dylan had believed about the booth, it was only the beginning.

And now, the booth was reaching for him...

CHAPTER THIRTY-ONE

The Choice Paradox

About the Author: Vaidehi Singh
I'm Vaidehi Singh, an 18-year-old from the spiritual city of Varanasi. I believe that life is a collection of moments we only get to experience once, so I strive to embrace each one to its fullest. As an extrovert, I love connecting with people and find joy in listening to music. Gazing at the stars and sky fills me with a sense of wonder. Writing serves as my outlet to express my thoughts and experiences, and I hope to inspire others to see the beauty in life.

*****

"Can it get any worse?" I sighed, slumping onto the terrace swing. The cool breeze brushed my face, a rare moment of peace amid the chaos that was my day. I was supposed to wake up early to study. My plan included meditating or going for a walk. Finals were just two months away, and I'd decided to start revising. But that was my *plan*, not my routine.

Instead, I woke up just an hour before school and rushed through everything. To make matters worse, I got my test results back and barely passed. Now here I am, wondering, "Where did I go wrong?" This wasn't the first time either—nothing this semester had gone the way I planned.

It felt like I was stuck in a loop, spiraling downward. Forget a "glow-up"; this was definitely my "glow-down" era.

I was supposed to be in extra classes right now, but I skipped. Sitting here, I tried to justify it as needing fresh air, but even to me, it sounded like a weak excuse.

"Am I not serious enough about the dreams I've always had? Should I pity myself for lacking self-control, or for being unable to make proper decisions?" My thoughts swirled.

"Maybe I'm just bad at this game of life," I muttered.

"Wait... no. I didn't say that. Did I?"

A chill ran down my spine. It was as if someone else had whispered it. Before I could look around, a sharp force struck my back, and I lurched forward. There was no time to scream, no time to process. The solid terrace tiles beneath me were gone, replaced by open air.

I was falling.

The wind roared in my ears as my body twisted mid-air. My arms flailed, searching for something to grab, but there was only emptiness. *How long does it take to fall fifteen stories?* A thought flickered through my mind, absurd in its calmness. *Is this what dying feels like?*

I closed my eyes, bracing for impact.

Suddenly, I jolted awake.

My heart pounded as I sat up in bed, drenched in sweat. My clock glowed faintly—3:15 AM. The room was dark and quiet, but my mind raced. The fall—it had felt so real. I tried to convince myself it was just a dream.

Then came the sound.

Glass shattering.

I froze, my heart thudding in my chest. The noise echoed through the empty house. A realization struck me like ice water: I was alone. My parents were out of town for the week.

The sound came from upstairs—from the kitchen. Someone had broken in.

Panic surged through me. I needed to get out. Trembling, I moved towards the front door. My breath came in short gasps as I reached the stairs. Then I heard it: the kitchen door opening with a violent thud. Footsteps—heavy, deliberate, getting louder, moving toward me.

They weren't cautious footsteps, the kind you'd expect from a burglar. They were loud, fast, and predatory.

They were coming for *me*.

I bolted for the door, stumbling outside into the night. I ran through the yard, my heart pounding in my ears. Behind me, a shadow pursued, gaining ground. In the distance, headlights blazed—a bus. The light grew blinding, and then—blackness.

I gasped awake, sitting up in bed once again. My heart hammered as I realized it had all been a dream. Again. But this time, a sense of dread settled over me.

The clock.

I was late.

Rushing through my morning, I ignored the uneasy feeling that followed me. It lingered, a whisper in the back of my mind: *I've seen this before.*

After another exhausting day at school, I found myself on the terrace again. Frustration boiled over—missed assignments, failed tests, skipped classes. The weight of my failures pressed on me. Then, the déjà vu hit, heavy and cold.

"Maybe I'm not playing this game of life properly," I murmured. But those weren't my words. Someone else had said them.

And then it happened—that sharp shove.

I was falling.

This time, I wasn't surprised. I knew how it would end. The blackness came, and when I woke, I was drenched in sweat, the same nightmare replaying itself. The glass shattered again.

But this time, something clicked.

"Maybe I'm not playing this game of life properly."

The words echoed in my mind, clearer now. This wasn't random. It was a message.

Life is a game. My choices are the moves; the outcomes are the consequences. If I wanted to escape this loop, I couldn't keep making the same choices. I had to play differently.

The next morning, I woke with a sense of purpose. I got ready earlier than usual, pushing through the exhaustion. At school, I didn't hide in the back of the class. I faced the extra assignments I'd been avoiding.

It felt strange, like stepping into someone else's life. But by the end of the day, something was different. Lighter. The weight of my mistakes was lifting.

And for once, I didn't find myself drifting back to the terrace.

I wasn't at the edge anymore—figuratively or literally.

Life is a game, and I'm finally playing it right.

CHAPTER THIRTY-TWO

Weeping Willows

About the Author: Vedika Mishra
Born on November 11, 2008, in Varanasi, Vedika Mishra has always been a natural communicator. Encouraged by her father, a businessman, and her storytelling mother, she thrived in public speaking, debate, and school performances from a young age. Throughout her academic journey, Vedika became a key figure in debate teams, oratory competitions, and student councils, sharpening her skills in leadership and communication. With a passion for inspiring others, she continues to excel as a dynamic and engaging speaker.

*****

The small town of Eldewood lay nestled in a valley, encompassed by tall hills and lush forests. In the heart of the village square, which hosted any major event, either joyful or sad, rows of tall ancient willow trees with sweeping branches stood like graceful green curtains. Through ages past, they had silently borne witness to stories of a lifetime of love and sorrow, life and death. Every weeping willow was testimony to a union—a bond sealed by time and tradition. Centuries flew by, but the custom continued unabated: with each marriage, a willow tree was planted on the edges of the Eldewood River. People said that these trees granted a newlywed couple long life, happiness, and well-being. It was the town's most cherished tradition, as deep in its people as those trees were in the earth. Underneath their beauty, though, underneath the soft leaves that whispered, one found a very ancient, evil curse—one that nobody really talked about. Elders would sometimes refer to it in the most guarded of tones, warning others of its dangers. Mara and Owen were young, so in love, knowing each other since childhood and playing in the shadow of the willows, weaving magic and wonder into children's games.

They had spent languid afternoons as teenagers under the trees, their fingers interlaced as they planned their futures together. It was Mara's laugh that had always quickened Owen's heartbeat, and Owen's silent strength that had always been Mara's anchor in times of doubt. They were meant to marry; they had always said it themselves. With the announcement of their engagement, the town rejoiced, and preparations for their wedding began almost immediately. It was going to be a common custom to plant a willow tree in their name after the ceremony. The idea sent Mara into ecstasies. She liked the thought of how their love would live in this town forever, stronger with each passing year, just like the growth of the trees around them. Then one evening, while they sat beneath the largest of the willows, Owen chanced upon an old, weathered book in the town library—which spoke of the ancient tradition buried beneath the legends of love and prosperity.

It was the willows, an elders' utopian curse, whereby every couple the willows blessed was forced to pay a price. For one to live long and prosper, the other had to die. At first, he did not believe it; to him, the book seemed more a story than a record of fact. How could something so beautiful hide horror? But he followed the trail of history further and discovered unexplained deaths: young spouses, in the flower of health, dying suddenly without explanation; elders whose partners had perished, living on into remarkable old age and dying rich and blessed. It was a pattern too clear to be ignored. One evening, Owen confided in Mara about his findings. She had laughed at first, passing it off as a folktale; still, as Owen continued, a chill crept down her spine. The trees—the very ones they had loved for so long—seemed darker now, their graceful branches concealing shadows they had never seen before. "You think it's true?" Mara asked with a shaking voice. Owen hesitated. "I don't know. But what if it is?" Mara said, piercing into his eyes, her heart in conflict. "Owen, I don't want to live a long life without you. What's the point in prosperity if you are not beside me? If this curse is real, we have to find a way to break it." And so, it was decided that night—to break the curse and stand together against it come whatever may. They knew it then and believed it now: true, unbreakable love can conquer any curse. They married anyway. The day was brilliant: the sky a brilliant blue, the willow branches dancing in the wind with grace, and the whole town present and accounted for to bless their union. After the ceremony, as was custom, townsfolk repaired to the riverbank. The place for their willow tree had been chosen, and it was a little sapling, ready to be planted. Mara and Owen stood hand in hand, gazing at the young tree. For a moment, the world seemed to hold its breath. The soft murmur of the river, the rustle of the trees—everything seemed alive with expectation.

The sapling was planted, and as people in the town cheered, Mara and Owen looked at each other. Yet, they both knew that the weight of that curse pressed down upon them beneath their smiles, and neither wished to give that curse any credence. Together, they'd break it—together they would survive. Blissful were the first several months of their marriage. They moved in together in a cozy cottage on the outskirts of the town, near the willow grove where they had spent so many afternoons together. Life felt perfect. Mara painted and tended the garden, while Owen worked in the town's wood shop. They were content, and for a time, they almost forgot about the curse. Yet, strange things started to happen. Mara began to dream in technicolor detail. She'd walk among the willow trees, their limbs tangling above her head, whispering in a language she couldn't understand. Always, she found herself drawn to one particular tree: the one planted for her and Owen. Its leaves were darker than the others, and it seemed that its branches reached for her, pulling her near. One night, Mara awoke startled; Owen was not lying beside her. Panicked, she ran outside, calling his name. She found him standing by their willow tree, his face pale, his eyes unfocused. "Owen!" she cried, running to him. He turned to her slowly, as if he were coming out of some dream. "I... I don't know what I'm doing here," he whispered. "I woke up and I just... I couldn't stop walking." Mara clutched his arm. "We have to go, get as far away from this place as possible. The curse... it's real, Owen. I can feel it." But Owen shook his head. "We can't leave, Mara. The tree is bound to us. We can't run from it."

Days soon drowned into weeks, and the tension between them started to rise. Mara's dreams got heavier, scarier. She started to hear whispers even when she was awake, and every time she looked at their willow tree, she felt a growing sense of dread. One night, after an unusually acrid nightmare, Mara made up her mind: she'd visit the tree and stare right in the face whatever force tried to tear them apart. She couldn't let it take Owen, not when they had fought so hard to stay together. As she approached the tree, the air around her seemed to grow colder. The wind picked up, and the willow branches swayed in protest, as if violently agitated. She stood before the tree, her heart racing, and spoke aloud. "I know what you are," she said, her voice trembling but firm. "You won't take him from me. You won't take us. We'll break your curse." For a moment, the wind died, and the world fell eerily silent. Then, with a sudden gust, the tree's branches lashed out, wrapping around Mara like a living thing. She screamed, but her voice was swallowed by the wind. Owen, who'd been asleep inside, woke with a start. He sprinted out into the garden, his heart racing, to find Mara wrapped in the branches of the tree, tugging with all her might. Of course, he ran to her without a second thought, pulling at the branches in an attempt to pull her to safety. But as his hands touched the bark, a strange energy coursed through him.

The whispers grew loud—deafening in his ears—and he knew in that instant the curse could never be broken. One of them had to die. Realization hit him like a blow; he had thought they could defy the curse, but it had been foolish of him to think that they could escape fate. There and then, Owen decided upon something. He looked at Mara with wide, frightened eyes and said in a whisper, "I love you." Before Mara could utter anything in response, Owen tore the branches off her and flung himself into the tree's embrace. The branches constricted and sucked him within their grasp, and Mara screamed as she saw him disappear into darkness. The next morning, the city found Mara slumped at the bottom of the willow tree, wailing uncontrollably. Owen was gone, his body never recovered.

People whispered to each other, speculating what happened, but none of them dared go close to the tree. Mara lived on, haunted by the memory of Owen's sacrifice. It was the curse, just as it had been for so many others. Her days were filled with a quiet solitude, tending the garden they built, her heart heavy with grief. The willow tree grew tall and strong, arcing low to the ground. A silent reminder of love now lost and the price they paid. Though Mara would live many years, prosper, and be blessed by the curse as it had promised, she never forgot the cost of her survival. Underneath the willow tree, Owen's spirit stayed to watch over her, silently guarding the legacy of love and loss that bound them. And the trees went on whispering their songs in the wind, and the town of Eldewood kept planting its trees, wholly oblivious to the evil that stirred below their roots.

Non-Fiction

Narratives & Descriptives

Ahead lies a collection of reflections drawn from real-life experiences, heartfelt truths, and insightful observations. These narratives are raw, authentic, and deeply personal, offering glimpses into the lives and minds of the authors. With every story, you'll discover a piece of the world as they see it, reminding us that reality often carries the greatest inspiration.

CHAPTER THIRTY-THREE

My First Debate

About the Author: Gauri Singh

Gauri is a twelfth-grader with a passion for creative writing and debating. Her interest in writing began during the COVID lockdown- when she started experimenting with blogging. She eventually began a blog 'Brighter Alleys', where she enjoys reflecting on everyday experiences.

Balancing the demands of school life as a JEE aspirant, she finds solace in journaling and dancing. She has even learned Bharatnatyam for thirteen years!

*****

I have always been fascinated by speeches. Listening to great personalities articulate their ideas with charisma and passion has always been an enriching experience for me. The art of debating, in particular, holds a special place in my heart. It is not just a means of argumentation but a powerful tool to shape opinions, inspire change, and open minds. Ever since I was in seventh grade, I had a burning desire to participate in debates and experience that electrifying exchange of ideas. Unfortunately, the lockdown over the next two years kept that dream on hold.

It wasn't until Class X that an opportunity finally came knocking. An inter-house debate competition was announced, and I knew this was my chance to step forward. My excitement, however, was quickly overshadowed by a creeping sense of fear. "Can I do it well?" was the first thought that invaded my mind. I was a complete novice, and the thought of speaking before an audience made my palms sweat. Yet, I reminded myself of the adage: *opportunity knocks but once.* With that in mind, I gathered all my courage and submitted my name.

That day, as I returned home, I knew I had a mountain of work ahead of me. The topic I was assigned was "Social media is harmful to the peace of a country." It was time to dig deep—gather statistics, quotes, news articles, and any relevant data to build a compelling argument. Hours of online searching yielded little, but I didn't lose hope. I knew Rome wasn't built in a day, and neither would my debate preparation be. Over the next few weeks, I poured myself into the task. I scoured the internet for insights, jotted down compelling points, and practiced speaking in front of the mirror, mimicking the confidence I had always admired in seasoned speakers.

Soon, the big day arrived. My heart was pounding as I entered the auditorium. The atmosphere was charged with excitement, the audience of about 600 students murmuring in anticipation. The debate began with speakers from the Yellow House, followed by the Blue House, and then the Red House—it was finally my turn. My badge read "F7," and as I adjusted the mic, I felt a surge of nervous energy coursing through me. But I reminded myself of a simple mantra: *All is well.* With that, I began.

I passionately defended my stance on the topic, pouring my heart into every word. In hindsight, I realize I was a bit too aggressive at the mic and used far too many hand gestures—a mistake that later cost me a few points. But in that moment, I was fully immersed in the experience. Five minutes flew by, and soon, it was time for the rebuttal round. I don't remember the exact question I was asked, but I do remember my rather silly response—somehow, I ended up comparing social media to a pizza! It wasn't my finest moment, but I carried on with as much composure as I could muster.

When my turn was over, I stepped down to a thunderous applause. It was a surreal moment. The 600 people in the audience—my classmates and juniors—didn't judge me for my mistakes. Instead, they encouraged me with their claps and cheers. For the first time, the vast sea of faces felt less intimidating and more like family.

As the competition neared its end, the results were announced. My heart raced as the Chair began naming the winners, starting with the third-place award. I hoped to hear my name, but not for third—I wanted to do better. When the Chair moved to the second-place award in the "For" category, she announced: "F7." That was me! A wave of elation washed over me as the applause erupted once again. I couldn't stop smiling.

It has been two years since that event, and it remains one of the most transformative experiences of my life. I have since participated in several other debates, each time improving and learning something new. One of the most valuable lessons I've learned is that debating is not about aggression or raising your voice. It's about presenting your views persuasively, with clarity and poise. I once came across a quote that beautifully encapsulates this idea: *"Raise your words, not your voice. It is rain that grows flowers, not thunder."* These words have stayed with me, guiding my approach to public speaking.

Looking back, I realize how important it is to step out of one's comfort zone and embrace co-curricular activities. That first debate was a stepping stone—it taught me courage, resilience, and the importance of preparation. Today, I no longer fear speaking in public. I have gained the confidence to voice my opinions and engage in meaningful discussions.

Had I not dared to take that first step, I might still be sitting in the audience, dreaming of what could have been. Instead, I chose to take a leap of faith, and it made all the difference.

CHAPTER THIRTY-FOUR

Colors of Life

About the Author: Gyanika Singh
Gyanika took her first step on 10 November 2008. She is an enthusiastic explorer. She loves to paint and likes to read books. She is very fond of "Nature". She has true friends, just like the adventure books...

*****

When I think about the colors of life, my mind drifts to the vivid hues of a rainbow—a natural masterpiece that symbolizes hope and harmony. The bright blue sky effortlessly captures my gaze, and the hot yellow sun warms my face, sometimes a little too fiercely. The forests are lush and green, brimming with life, as fresh as the dew-kissed grass in the early hours. This time of the year, even the mangoes radiate their golden brilliance, adding yet another shade to nature's palette.

But then, I look at us—humans. So many are glued to their smartphones, blind to the beauty of the world around them. The colors of life are all around us, yet we scroll through screens, oblivious. A handful might pause to take a picture of nature, sharing it on social media as a badge of aesthetic appreciation. But do they truly *feel* the beauty of what they capture? I don't think so.

And what of the holy river Ganga? Once revered for its purity, it now bears the burden of our neglect, polluted and crying for help. Cars, bikes, and endless industries add to the chaos, polluting the air we breathe and the lands we tread. Even students, who once learned by observing the world around them, now spend their precious hours playing games on smartphones, disconnected from the very lessons life and nature have to offer.

Reflecting on the past, I see a stark difference. There was a time when people cherished nature, when the simple joys of fresh water, crisp morning air, and the songs of birds brought happiness to their lives. Nature was unspoiled, its beauty untouched by pollutants. But now, everywhere I turn, there's pollution—on land, in water, and in the air.

We're cutting down trees, poisoning rivers, and suffocating the earth with our carelessness. The result? Diseases like dengue, malaria, and typhoid have become rampant. Yet, many people remain unaware or indifferent to the consequences of their actions.

But all is not lost. If we pause to think about the situation, we can realize the damage we've done and, more importantly, find solutions. Imagine a world where our mother earth is clean, where rivers sparkle with life, and the air is as pure as a child's laughter. How safe, how beautiful, how fulfilling our lives would be!

Schemes and promises are made to clean our planet, but look around—is it really happening? The answer is often no. But that doesn't mean we should give up. If we truly commit to change, our mother earth can regain her lost glory. Imagine a world where we don't just survive but thrive amidst the vibrant colors of life—a world where nature heals and flourishes.

So, let's put aside our smartphones and reconnect with the world around us. Let's spend time with the true colors of life. Let's find solutions, take action, and preserve the beauty that surrounds us.

"The rain itself has no color,
But it transforms parched, bronze grass
Into a vivid emerald green.
The colors of life are everywhere—
In nature, in memories, and even in dreams."
-Ruskin Bond

All we need to do is look.

CHAPTER THIRTY-FIVE

The Destination is Worth The Journey

About the Author: Tanishka Singh
Born on December 24, 2008, I have a deep passion for the Indian defense forces, particularly the Army and Paramilitary special forces. My academic journey encompasses skills in art, literature, and sports. Inspirational books like Atomic Habits by James Clear and The Great Oceans Within Us by Killada Satyanarayana have profoundly influenced my perspective. Field Marshal Sam Manekshaw stands as a significant inspiration in my life, helping me cultivate a strong work ethic, creativity, and a genuine passion for my pursuits.

*****

As I awoke to the soothing sound of my mother's voice, a sense of warmth and comfort enveloped me, offering a brief reprieve from the daunting challenges that awaited me as a 10th-grade student. The weight of expectations—both my own and my family's—often felt overwhelming. Yet, I remained resolute in my aspiration to join the Defence Services of India, a goal that had been a beacon of hope and determination in my life. The exemplary qualities of honour, courage, and intelligence displayed by the officers of the Defence Services served as a constant source of inspiration, lighting my path even during the darkest of times.

One of the most defining moments of my journey came when I was selected as the best cadet from Uttar Pradesh for the prestigious Republic Day camp. This incredible opportunity allowed me to interact with some of the most esteemed dignitaries of our nation, including the Prime Minister, the Vice President, the Defence Minister, and the Chiefs of the Army, Navy, Air Force, and Defence Staff. Standing in the presence of such accomplished leaders filled me with a profound sense of purpose and commitment. Yet, despite these significant experiences, I was acutely aware of the areas in which I needed to grow. My greatest challenge was to overcome my negative personality traits—my short temper, ego, and selfishness—and transform them into qualities of selflessness, humility, and empathy.

As a young woman aspiring to join the Defence Services, I faced societal expectations that often clashed with my ambitions. The journey was anything but easy, yet I remained steadfast and unwavering, recognizing that my calling lay in a field that demanded uncommon courage and sacrifice. During this time, I discovered my role model: Field Marshal Sam Manekshaw. His remarkable legacy, marked by exceptional leadership and an unyielding commitment to the nation, became a guiding light for me. Although he is no longer with us, his actions and values continue to leave an indelible mark on my life. Inspired by his example, I felt a deep desire to contribute meaningfully to the country, ready to make sacrifices for the greater good.

To achieve my goals, I understood the necessity of improving my character. I began keeping a diary, meticulously documenting my habits, mistakes, and areas for improvement. This practice proved transformative, fostering self-awareness and personal growth. Determined to eliminate distractions, I made the conscious decision to distance myself from social media and instead focused on cultivating discipline. I committed to waking up at 4:00 a.m. every day for 21 consecutive days, a practice that eventually became a lasting habit. While consistency is often easy to preach but difficult to maintain, I learned that each skipped day only delayed my progress toward my dreams.

Academically, my journey was a rollercoaster. Despite scoring an impressive 92% in my board exams, I faced a humbling setback when I failed my 11th-grade half-yearly examinations. The criticism and disappointment from those around me took a toll on my confidence, and I began to doubt myself. Looking back, I realize this failure stemmed from my complacency—I had assumed that the same level of effort would suffice after my previous success. However, this experience taught me the importance of perseverance. I redoubled my efforts and ultimately passed my 11th-grade annual examinations with a respectable 75%. In 12th grade, I worked harder than ever before and secured the top position on the board with an outstanding 98%.

The path to the National Defence Academy was no less challenging. I faced numerous hurdles during the written entrance examination and the Service Selection Board (SSB) interview process. Failing 12 times was emotionally draining, and the stress took a toll on my health. Yet, I refused to give up. On my 13th attempt, I finally achieved the remarkable feat of securing an all-India rank. That moment was one of immense pride and relief, but I remained grounded, fully aware that this was only the beginning. The road ahead would be even more demanding.

Life at the Academy was grueling yet transformative. Every day brought its own set of challenges, with competition present in every sphere—from academics and sports to drills and extracurricular events. Despite the intensity, I forged lifelong friendships with cadets from all across the country. These friendships became my pillars of strength, teaching me the value of camaraderie and teamwork. Our seniors, though tough, instilled in us the importance of collective responsibility. I recall how even a single cadet's mistake would result in the entire group being held accountable. This discipline taught me valuable lessons about leadership and unity.

Our daily routine at the Academy was rigorous. We spent 2 to 4 hours on sports, followed by 5 to 6 hours of academic classes, and another 2 to 3 hours on drill practice. The drill sessions were particularly intense, with our instructor allowing no room for errors or relaxation. Yet, amidst the relentless schedule, my friends and I found joy in the fleeting moments of camaraderie, recognizing their irreplaceable nature. The words of our seniors were often harsh, their intent to toughen us up for the challenges ahead. I vividly remember my drill instructor once asking me, "We make men out of boys; what should we make out of you?" Without hesitation, I replied with confidence, "An officer."

The training, hardships, and relentless challenges I faced at the Academy have shaped me into the person I am today. Each obstacle was a stepping stone, preparing me for the honor of bearing stars on my shoulders—an achievement I hold dearer than the stars in the sky. Looking back, I am filled with gratitude for every experience, every setback, and every triumph that has brought me to this point. The journey has not been easy, but it has been profoundly rewarding, and I am ready to face whatever lies ahead with courage and determination.

Escape Through Ink

About the Author: Venya Gujrati

I'm Venya Gujrati, and I believe that words have the power to make or break a moment. Writing became my refuge when life felt uncertain, transforming chaos into something beautiful. I view stories as both escapes and tools to challenge reality, allowing me to explore new possibilities. Quirky, curious, and a bit of a daydreamer, I am always in search of the next adventure within the ordinary. After all, why settle for less when you can rewrite the world?

*****

"We write to taste life twice, in the moment and in retrospect."

—Anaïs Nin

I remember the first time I wrote something that truly mattered to me. It wasn't for a school assignment or to impress anyone. It was a desperate attempt to make sense of the world that was crumbling around me. I was twelve, sitting at my desk with a spiral notebook that I had gotten as a birthday gift. There was something about the blank page that both terrified and excited me, like the way you feel before diving into cold water. The pen felt foreign in my hand at first, but soon, the words began to flow. It wasn't poetry, nor was it a story. It was something else entirely—a release.

Writing had found me. Or maybe I had found it.

It didn't take long for the notebook to become my refuge. Every day after school, I'd retreat to my room, shutting out the chaos of the world around me. At the time, my parents were going through a messy divorce. They thought they were protecting me from the details, but I could feel the tension in the air. It weighed heavy, like a thunderstorm that never quite broke but always threatened to. Writing became my way of coping. When words felt too sharp to say aloud, I whispered them to the page. I wasn't brave enough to tell my parents how scared I was or how much I hated the silence that had settled between them. But I was brave enough to write about it.

As I grew older, writing evolved from a way of processing my emotions to something much deeper. It became a form of escape, not just from the world but from myself. I wasn't running away; I was running toward something—a version of myself that was unafraid. In the stories I wrote, I was anyone and everyone. I was the hero who slayed dragons, the adventurer who discovered hidden worlds, and the poet who found meaning in the mundane. On paper, I was limitless.

What fascinated me most was how writing could take me anywhere. On days when life felt too ordinary, I'd disappear into the pages of a fantastical realm I created. There I could fly, wield magic, or speak to creatures no one else could see. On darker days, I wrote stories that mirrored my pain. I poured my heart into characters who were lost and broken but always searching for redemption. In some ways, writing was a mirror—a reflection of everything I was too scared to say out loud. But it was also a window, offering me glimpses into worlds that felt far kinder than my own.

Here's the thing about writing that no one tells you: it doesn't just help you escape. It heals.

It's funny. I had always thought of writing as my way out, a secret door I could slip through whenever the world became too much. But as the years passed, I realized that writing wasn't just an escape route—it was a way back in. Back into myself. Back into life.

Writing taught me to be brave. Not in the loud, heroic way we often see in movies, but in a quieter, more profound way. It taught me to sit with my emotions instead of running from them. It taught me to find beauty in the mess, in the fragments of life that don't quite fit together. Through my words, I learned that pain and joy aren't opposites. They exist side by side, often tangled up in ways that make them inseparable. And somehow, that makes the joy even sweeter.

There's something oddly magical about putting pen to paper. It's as if the act itself permits you to feel everything you've been holding back. The pen becomes an extension of your soul, spilling out all the things you didn't even know you were carrying. Writing is both liberating and terrifying. It asks you to be honest, not just with your readers but with yourself. And that kind of honesty, well, it changes you.

As I continued to write, I realized that the stories I was telling weren't just about imaginary worlds or fictional characters. They were about me. Every character I created and every plot twist I engineered was a reflection of my struggles, hopes, and dreams. Writing became a way of understanding myself, of piecing together the parts of me that didn't quite make sense. In the worlds I created, I found clarity.

But here's the quirky part—writing also has a strange way

of holding a mirror to the world. It lets you see things you might have missed. Like how the smallest moments—the flutter of a bird's wings, the way the light hits the trees at dusk, the sound of laughter echoing down a hallway—carry so much weight. Writing makes you pay attention—really pay attention—to the world around you. It slows you down, pulls you out of the rush, and invites you to notice the details. And in those details, you find meaning.

It's no exaggeration to say that writing saved me. Not in some grand, cinematic way, but in the quiet moments when I felt lost and writing was the only thing that made sense. It gave me a place to retreat, a place to heal, and, ultimately, a way to re-enter the world with a little more courage and a lot more compassion.

Now, I write for many reasons. I write to remember, to forget, to dream, to reflect. I write because, in a world that often feels overwhelming, words are the only thing I can control. I write because it's my way of making sense of the chaos and of finding beauty in the brokenness. I write because, through stories, I can escape—but more importantly, I can come back, a little braver than before.

So, if you ever feel like the world is spinning too fast or too slow, or you're just not sure where you fit in—write. Write about the things that scare you, the things that make you laugh, and the things that keep you up at night. Write, not for anyone else, but for you. Because in those words, you'll find your escape. And in that escape, you might just find yourself.